HAUNTED
WEST END

HAUNTED
WEST END

Gilly Pickup

The History Press

To Mike,
for his input, encouragement
and reviving cups of coffee.

In memory of my mum.

First published 2013

The History Press
The Mill, Brimscombe Port
Stroud, Gloucestershire, GL5 2QG
www.thehistorypress.co.uk

British Library Cataloguing in Publication Data.
A catalogue record for this book is available from the British Library.

ISBN 978 0 7524 9943 7

Typesetting and origination by The History Press
Printed in Great Britain

CONTENTS

INTRODUCTION

Chances of bumping into an apparition in London's West End are high. In fact, this area of the capital, particularly popular with theatregoers and tourists, simply swirls with spirits. It has to be said that even though they lack a physical body, they certainly don't lack imagination. So while it's to be expected that they strut their stuff in houses old and new, they also haunt restaurants, hospitals, pubs, alleyways, police stations and even a bed. Spooky theatres? Yes, of course! Ghostly hotels? Absolutely. A haunted bank? That too.

This book brims over with true tales of eerie encounters, some of which are terrifying enough to capture the imagination of even the most hardened sceptic. After all, there are more reported uncanny happenings in this part of London than you can shake a spook at, most of which are guaranteed to make you look at the West End you are familiar with, either personally or through written accounts, in a totally different way.

Wallow in these scary tales of tortured souls and malevolent entities and encounter spirits of the famous including Napoleon III, who haunts the basement of one of London's busiest hotels.

Hear ghostly voices of children in a modern office block built over a plague pit and discover which theatre houses a female spectre who cradles a severed head in her lap. There are tales in this creepy collection which are guaranteed to make your blood run cold.

Read on, if you dare to find out:

Shaftesbury Avenue at night.
(VisitLondon images/Britain on View/Pawel Libera)

7

Who was the headless phantom exorcised from the bank vaults?

Why did a theatre prop cause bone-chilling fear?

Where have two people have been frightened to death – literally?

When did a spectre appear before a Prime Minister?

Now all you have to do is sit down, make yourself comfortable and savour these nerve-jangling tales. Make sure you have locked your windows and doors first though, and do well to remember that the dead in this part of London far outnumber the living.

Gilly Pickup, 2013

1

THE WEST END

The West End, so called because it is located to the west of the historic city of London, is the hub of one of the world's greatest cities.

This is where to find most of the capital's major tourist attractions, businesses and administrative headquarters. A host of neighbourhoods make up this part of London, weaving together major concentrations of art galleries, museums, hotels, media establishments, embassies, legal institutions, nightclubs, cinemas, bars, restaurants, shops and residential areas. However, what the West End is most renowned for is its theatre scene. London's West End is the largest theatre

Bond Street, West End. (westendmediacentre.com)

Theatreland. (Gilly Pickup)

district in the world. Indeed, the term 'West End' has become synonymous with London's commercial theatre. 'Theatreland' is home to forty-two internationally renowned theatres and many more non-profit organisations and producing houses. Like the Old Vic, some of these lie outside the geographical boundaries of Theatreland, but are still very much a part of its tradition.

This epicentre of London has no hard and fast boundaries, but generally speaking is mainly contained within the city of Westminster, one of the thirty-two London boroughs. The West End often refers to the whole of central London, itself an area with no generally agreed boundaries.

The stories in this book take the reader on a spooktacular journey that covers Holborn's Lincoln's Inn, the one-time site of public executions and said to be haunted by an evil executioner. Then there is intellectual Bloomsbury, home of the British Library and a weeping ghost. Compact, frenetic, once-sleazy Soho, oozing trendy bars, smart restaurants and encompassing dynamic,

bustling, colourful Chinatown also has its otherworldly side – no wonder, when you consider part of the area stands over a plague pit. Aristocratic, elegant Mayfair, named after the annual spring festival held until the 1730s, provides us with tales from two of London's spectacularly eerie haunted pubs, as well as the on-going mystery of what is surely London's most haunted house. St James's, which starts at Piccadilly and includes Green Park, has a couple of seriously scary phantoms that you wouldn't want to meet, while a poignant spectre haunts an embassy in swish Belgravia, one of the most expensive areas in the world. The many theatres in Covent Garden, Piccadilly, Leicester Square, Shaftesbury Avenue and Charing Cross are simply awash with mysterious spirits and strange goings-on. Marylebone, owned in the twelfth century by a brotherhood of warrior monks called the Knights Templar, has its phantoms too, including that of a famous actress; as does the once-bohemian Fitzrovia, which lies to the north-east of Oxford Circus and is where a plethora of hospital ghosts

Lincoln's Inn. (Gilly Pickup)

can be found. Familiar names all, that trip off the tongue whether you are a local, a visitor, or someone who knows London only from films and books.

I have loosely divided the stories into four regions: North, South, East and West. The boundaries are not fixed and there is some overlap because some sites have a linking theme. Logically, therefore, they are linked to others with that theme. However, with a little planning and the help of a street map, visitors and ghost hunters should be able to access a good number of sites in one day.

The West End is one of the busiest places in the world so anyone can be forgiven for thinking there are few dark corners, creepy buildings or nooks and crannies for the odd ghost to lurk. Who would expect to encounter a supernatural being in the middle of one of the world's greatest cities? But below and within these streets of modern London, embedded in the fabric of buildings and the streets themselves, are layers of mysteries of times gone by – memories and emotions of those no longer in our world.

That is why, without further ado, we'll leave behind the buzz, bustle and bright lights and set off to explore the West End's more mysterious, creepy side – that is, of course, if you are prepared to be scared!

2

NORTH

'Yesterday, upon the stair,
I met a man who wasn't there,
He wasn't there again today,
I wish that man would go away.'
    (*Antigonish* by Hughes Mearns)

Everyone loves a good ghost story, whether or not they actually believe in ghouls, ghosts and things that go bump in the night. You would not be reading this book otherwise. Even those with a cynical mind will admit to even just a wisp of worry about the supernatural, and there can be few among us who would look forward to meeting a ghost.

Let's start by taking a look at the presences which haunt some theatres in this part of London known as Theatreland.

Look Out Behind You!

Theatres can be spooky labyrinths at night after the audience has gone home. Everyone knows that actors are a superstitious and imaginative lot, with sayings about 'breaking a leg', squeaky shoes, no whistling allowed in dressing rooms and woe betide anyone who brings a peacock feather on stage.

Then there is the 'Scottish' play which I won't name but will only say that if an actor mistakenly lets the 'Mac★★★★' word slip in the dressing room, he or she must perform a ritual to reverse the curse.

A stage door. (Mike Pickup)

Although antics vary depending on whom you ask, the actor may have to run from the building, turn around three times, spit and then ask permission to come back into the theatre.

Many West End theatres have resident phantoms or documented reports of weird, otherworldly happenings. Some are humorous, some are definitely grisly, but there are a few which are simply terrifying. Others, meanwhile, have a sad story attached to them, as is the case of the spirits who haunt the Dominion Theatre.

Dominion Theatre, Tottenham Court Road

The theatre stands on the site of Meux's Horse Shoe Brewery, and over the years members of the audience have claimed to see a ghostly figure, thought to be that of a brewery worker, lurking in the wings. Occasionally, too, sounds of giggling children filter through empty dressing rooms while reports of poltergeist activity, involving objects which mysteriously disappear only to reappear elsewhere, may send a shiver down the spine.

But perhaps it is not surprising that this theatre should have an apparition or two because on 17 October 1814, a huge vat containing 3,550 barrels of beer – over a million pints – ruptured. The beer tsunami destroyed two houses and knocked down the wall of the Tavistock Arms pub in Great Russell Street.

The Times of 19 October reported:

The neighbourhood of St. Giles was thrown into the utmost consternation on Monday night, by one of the most melancholy accidents we ever remember. About six o'clock, one of the vats in the extensive premises of Messrs. Henry Meux

and Co., in Banbury-street, St. Giles burst, and in a moment New-street, George-street and several others in the vicinity were deluged with the contents, amounting to 3,500 barrels of strong beer. The fluid, in its course, swept everything before it. Two houses in New-street, adjoining the brew-house, were totally demolished.

A flood of alcohol swept the area, killing most of those in its path by drowning, injury, poisoning by porter fumes or, in the case of one man, simply from alcohol poisoning, such was his heroic attempt to stem the tide by drinking as much beer as he possibly could. One of the dead was a 14-year-old barmaid, Eleanor Cooper, and it is thought that she is one of those who comes back to haunt her former workplace. Staff and patrons have had numerous unusual experiences in this theatre – being aware of strange sensations, perhaps a gentle tapping on the shoulders, the fleeting touch of a hand, lights which flicker and fail, or even something which pushes through groups of visitors. The strange thing is, though they feel it, they cannot see what it is that is pushing past them.

The London Palladium, Argyll Street

Argyll Street was developed in the early 1730s, on land belonging to John Campbell, 2nd Duke of Argyll. His son, Archibald Campbell, 3rd Duke, built Argyll House in 1737, and from 1740–62 his mistress, Mrs Shireburn, lived here.

Originally, Argyll House occupied the site on which the London Palladium now stands, on the east side of Argyll Street. The Palladium has a rather colourful past. It started out as the Corinthian Bazaar, which featured an aviary, before it became a circus venue, the brainchild of Fredrick Hengler, son of a tightrope walker. After that it opened as the National Skating Palace, an ice rink, and when that did not succeed it was rebuilt as a theatre and called the Palladium.

Arguably, the most famous of the West End theatres, it was built in 1910, though the façade (that of Argyll House) dates back to the nineteenth century. Grade II listed by English Heritage in 1960, this theatre originally had its own telephone system so that the occupants of boxes could call one another; it had a revolving stage too – very high tech for the day.

Behind the Royal Circle there is a red staircase called, rather unimaginatively, the 'Old Crimson Staircase'. Before 1973, nothing unusual as far as paranormal goings-on were concerned seemed to occur in this theatre, or at least none were reported, but it was in that year that a female spectre dressed in a lemon-coloured crinoline made her first appearance. Since then she has emerged from time to time, and actors, usherettes and other theatre staff have seen her gliding past them, skirt rustling, as they ascend the stairs. This unassuming presence is thought to be Mrs Shireburn, the 3rd Duke's mistress.

Palace Theatre, Cambridge Circus

To conciliate spirits, the Palace Theatre keeps two seats in the balcony permanently bolted open to provide seating for the theatre ghosts. The shade of ballerina Anna Pavlova has occasionally appeared in this theatre also. Originally built as an opera house, the Palace Theatre was the venue for her first London performance, so it is perhaps apt that she should choose to return here from time to time.

Palace Theatre, London. (Matt May)

Visitors have reported seeing orbs of light coming from darkened areas at the rear left-hand side of the building followed by the vague shape of a female, assumed to be her. Some who have seen her say she is 'not quite white, but semi-transparent'.

The building's other entity is that of Ivor Novello, the Anglo-Welsh matinee idol, author and composer who died in 1951. Several actors and members of staff have encountered the spectre in the wings. Novello, who wrote 'Keep the Home Fires Burning', a song that expressed the feelings of innumerable families torn apart by the First World War, has also been spotted watching performances from the back of the dress circle. But don't worry, these presences are not frightening but simply add an extra soupçon of interest to a visit to the Palace Theatre.

Non-Theatrical Ghosts

Room 333, Langham Hotel, Portland Place

Foley House, the 3rd Lord Foley's London residence, used to stand on the spot where the Langham Hotel is today. The demise of Foley House came about when the family fortune was squandered

Langham Hotel. (Mike Pickup)

in 1814 and architect John Nash acquired the whole estate as settlement of a debt. The upshot was the house was demolished and the Langham Hotel, London's largest residential building and Europe's first 'Grand Hotel', was constructed in its place.

The Langham, an ostentatious building with gold and scarlet interiors lavish to the point of bombast, had 600 rooms and cost £300,000 to build – a huge sum in those days. Over 2,000 people, including HRH the Prince of Wales, who later became King Edward VII, attended the glittering gala opening on 10 June 1865.

Anyone staying at the Langham Hotel was automatically assumed to be of very high standing. Roll those credits for Mark Twain, Arnold Bennett, Arthur Conan Doyle, Noel Coward, Napoleon III, Gracie Fields, Charles Laughton,

Mrs Wallis Simpson and, more recently, Diana, Princess of Wales. The composer Dvorak once visited too, although he managed to offend the sensibilities of the management when, in an attempt to save money, he requested a double room for himself and his grown-up daughter. The hotel was also the setting for several of Arthur Conan Doyle's Sherlock Holmes stories, including the chilling Sign of Four.

Not only was the Langham the first hotel with state-of-the-art fire protection and hydraulic lifts, or 'rising rooms' as they were known, but it had – indeed, still has – another rather more sinister claim to fame as one of England's most haunted hotels. This hotel has somehow acquired several uninvited guests during its 148-year history, reportedly having up to seven ghosts.

Langham Hotel. (Mike Pickup)

The Langham encountered a blip when, as other grand hotels were built in the West End, its popularity waned and it closed down. When it reopened, it had a change of purpose and was used as administrative offices for the BBC. Several rooms on the third floor became staff quarters for those whose late finishes or early starts necessitated an overnight stay, and many sightings come from this time.

The spectre of a tall, silver-haired man dressed in a sweeping cloak and cravat sometimes frequents the hotel's upper floors. Although his description sounds harmless enough, those who have encountered him say he is 'a terrifying figure' with 'blank staring eyes'. Whispers are that he is the spirit of a doctor rumoured to have killed himself after murdering his wife while they honeymooned in the hotel. Exactly who he was, and why he murdered his wife, no one seems to know.

In another room, formerly a reference library in the days of the BBC, occupants have reported a sudden sharp drop in temperature which heralds the arrival of a footman dressed in blue livery, complete with powdered wig.

This eighteenth-century figure is thought to be a good-natured apparition from the days when Foley House stood here. It often happens that the ghosts of those from times gone by return to reclaim those places that they knew so well in life.

Several BBC personnel say they also experienced the antics of a mischievous spirit in Room 632, who had a habit of tipping sleeping night-shift staff out of their beds. Regular sightings continued over the years with the last recorded chilling experience in this room taking place in August 2002, when a guest found himself lying on the floor after 'something unseen but with a huge strength' pushed him out of bed.

There have also been sightings of a phantom butler wandering the corridors before dissolving into thin air, though he seems to have gone for good now as his apparition has not been witnessed, or at least reported, since 1974. There are a number of people, however, who have since observed the figure of a young woman in the same area. According to witnesses, the girl, who is dressed in a 'bluish gown, probably a nightdress', is thought to be the butler's girlfriend, but why she has replaced him is yet another mystery.

All well and spooky, but by far the most nerve-racking of all the inexplicable happenings in the Langham is the phantom of Room 333. Mock if you will, but it scares the living daylights out of most of those who check into that room.

In 1973, James Alexander Gordon, legendary reader of the football results on BBC Radio, awoke in the night to see a fluorescent ball hovering on the opposite side of the room. Slowly, it took on the shape of a man dressed in Victorian eveningwear. Summoning up his courage, the terrified presenter asked the apparition who it was and what it wanted. The question seemed to irritate it, and it began to float towards him, arms outstretched, staring at him maliciously. This was bad enough, but what made this sight more blood-curdling was that its legs seemed to be cut off from just below the knee. At this point, Gordon got up and fled. He went down to the commissionaire, who refused to accompany him back to the room. Gordon bravely returned alone and found his mysterious guest still present, although its appearance seemed less distinct than before. He shouted at the spirit, told it to get out and leave him alone before removing a shoe to throw it at it. The presence vanished, at least for the rest of the night. Later, when he told his colleagues at Broadcasting House about his ordeal, others told of seeing the apparition in the same room. Why did the ghoul look as if his legs were cut off? Because the floors had been raised since Victorian times, when central heating pipes were installed throughout the building.

But that isn't all the eerie goings-on in the Langham. A German prince who committed suicide by jumping from a fourth-floor window, just after the start of the First World War, has been seen quite often. Although his antics are not confined solely to Room 333, he seems to have a particular penchant for that room. The late BBC announcer Ray Moore, described him as 'beefy, with cropped hair, sporting a military-style jacket that buttoned up to the neck'. He has been observed several times in the early morning, walking through closed doors, and is rated the most active apparition at the hotel.

After the BBC moved out, the hotel had a glitzy makeover before being reopened by the Hilton Hotel Group in 1991, at a cost of £80 million. The building work didn't seem to deter the phantoms though. Emperor Napoleon III, who lived at the Langham during his last days in exile, still continues to haunt the basement, while a rather more disturbing sight of a apparition with a gaping wound on his face haunts the lower floor hallways late at night, causing fear and revulsion to those who happen upon him.

But, if you will, let's go back to Room 333. A guest told how a friend of hers saw the apparition in this room. Terrified, she screamed and, like James Alexander Gordon, hurled her shoe at it. It seemed as if the footwear passed right through the phantom but did not deter it as it kept moving towards her, its face contorted in a dreadful grimace.

In May 2003, a guest checked out of the hotel in a rush very late one night without giving any reason for her premature departure. A few days later she sent a letter to the management explaining that her slumbers had been interrupted by the activities of a spectre who kept her from her sleep by repeatedly shaking the bed during the night.

Why is this room apparently haunted by so many apparitions? Is it because the number 333 represents the Holy Trinity? Is it because when doubled, it is the number of the devil? Or is it because 3 a.m. is the demonic witching hour, and of all the minutes in that hour, 3.33 a.m. is considered by some to be the devil's favourite time of day? Perhaps we will never know.

So, those cynical people, or even those who just want to take the chance of being scared rigid, may request to stay in Room 333, subject to availability. One thing is certain though; I know I wouldn't … would you?

Broadcasting House, Portland Place

Returning to the BBC, let's take a quick look inside Broadcasting House, a mere hop, skip and jump from the Langham Hotel and apparently the stamping ground of some spine-chilling lost souls.

In the 1930s, staff often saw a handlebar mustachioed man dressed in eighteenth-century clothes limping around the fourth floor of the building. Witnesses thought he must be a member of the management until to their utter shock he started to fade away before their eyes. Since then, members of staff have also reported sightings of a phantom waiter, a frightening picture in the extreme – those unfortunate

BBC's Portland Place. (Mike Pickup)

enough to encounter him are horrified to see that where his eyes should be there are only two blank, black sockets. Another wraith-like figure occasionally hovers around the corridors. This is a musician who looks very real but troubled. Staff have approached the man who carries a violin – to ask if they can help – but he simply smiles, shakes his head and disappears.

Lincoln's Inn Fields, High Holborn

In the sixteenth and seventeenth centuries, London's largest public square was a major site of public executions. Lincoln's Inn Fields was a popular place in those days; after all, an execution was seen by the masses as a good day out, rather like a visit to a theme park might be nowadays. This story is about two well-known men of their time, who were executed here and who have both returned in spirit.

In 1586, Anthony Babington and thirteen co-conspirators were convicted of high treason and sentenced to be hanged, drawn and quartered for their part in the plot to remove Queen Elizabeth I from the throne of England

BBC's Portland Place. (Mike Pickup)

Lincoln's Inn Fields. (Gilly Pickup)

and replace her with Mary, Queen of Scots. In fact, the 'Babington Plot' and Mary's involvement in it were the basis of the treason charges against her which led to her execution.

Because there were so many of them, and the manner of execution was lengthy as well as ghastly, it was decided that the executions would take place over two days. The first seven would be executed, watched by the second seven. Because the conspirators sometimes met in the area of Lincoln's Inn Fields, this was seen as an appropriate place for them to die. However, the screams of terror from the first seven as they underwent unspeakable torture rent the air for miles around and drew public sympathy, so the Queen ruled that the second group should be executed in a

more straightforward way. Among the first group were Anthony Babington, John Ballard and Chidiock Tichborne.

Another man of note, Lord William Russell, son of the first Duke of Bedford, was beheaded here in 1683 for the attempted assassination of King Charles II. Russell's executioner was the gruesome Jack Ketch, who made such a poor job of it that it required four axe blows before the head was separated from the body. Allegedly, after the first stroke, Russell looked up and said to him, 'You dog, did I give you 10 guineas to use me so inhumanely?' The name 'Jack Ketch' is now a proverbial name for death – a real life bogeyman.

The wailing wraith of Anthony Babington, and occasionally the shade of William Russell, sometimes roam

Lincoln's Inn Fields. (Gilly Pickup)

the grounds at night, so some folks say. Less surprisingly, the phantom of nasty fellow Jack Ketch also prowls round the square after dark, mainly on summer evenings when the moon slips out. It is perhaps wise to stay well out of his way.

University College Hospital, Gower Street

There are plenty of old hospitals in the UK; many have at least one and sometimes several ghost stories attached to them. In his lifetime, veteran ghost hunter Andrew Green collected dozens of stories of hospital hauntings. Stories vary, but a common theme is a 'Grey Lady' or 'Woman in White', who made a serious medical error and then committed suicide, only to reappear at times of crisis. Green believed that these apparitions are forms of electromagnetic energy, a faded echo of people whose lives were intensely stressful.

For this particular tale, we go to University College Hospital. Besides being known for its spooks, it is noted as being the first hospital to have an operation

carried out with the use of a general anaesthetic. On 21 December 1846, Dr Robert Liston, a Scot known as the 'fastest knife in Britain', amputated butler Frederick Churchill's leg in a record twenty-eight seconds; it was the first operation to be carried out in Britain using anaesthesia. Liston was used to operating quickly, at a time when speed made a difference in terms of pain and survival. He held the scalpel in his teeth while sewing. However, though speed was doubtless of the essence, a story which is perhaps fictional tells that in his hurry to perform a thigh amputation, Liston once 'included two fingers of his assistant and both testes of his patient'.

One of this hospital's spectres is that of a young nurse, Lizzie Church, who attended the bedside of her lover who was a patient in the 1890s. She accidentally killed him with a morphine overdose then committed suicide in remorse. Her presence still occasionally appears to hospital staff as a reminder to be careful when morphine is administered to patients.

Lizzie isn't the only apparition to haunt UCH though. Philosopher and social reformer Jeremy Bentham, hailed as 'the first patron saint of animal rights' and who died in 1832, has been seen following staff around the hospital, sometimes waving his walking stick at them. Incidentally, he gave all of his walking sticks names, and this one was called 'Dapple'. In his will, he specified that when he died he was to be dissected in the presence of friends and that his remains should be preserved and kept always in the college grounds.

Gruesome? Perhaps, but that was precisely what happened and the skeleton and head were preserved and stored in a wooden cabinet. The skeleton, which was given a wax head fitted with some of Bentham's own hair, was padded out with hay and dressed in Bentham's clothes. It was acquired by University College London in 1850 and is normally kept on public display at the end of the South Cloisters in the main building of the college.

Bentham had originally intended that his head should be part of the Auto-Icon (placed at UCL), but when the time came to preserve it, the process went disastrously wrong, robbing the head of most of its facial expression and leaving it decidedly unattractive. Nevertheless, it was displayed in the same case as the Auto-Icon for many years, on the floor between Bentham's legs, but became the target of repeated student pranks. Once it was stolen and held to ransom for charity, and on another occasion, students again stole it and it was later found in a luggage locker at a station. It is now locked away securely.

A portrait of Marcus Beck, a surgeon at University College Hospital in the mid-1800s, hung on a wall until it was stolen in 2001. It was considered to be a cursed picture because anyone who fell asleep under the painting quickly took a turn for the worse and in some cases died. Besides that, if the shutters were not closed on the painting at night, a patient would unexpectedly die.

University College Hospital New Building. ('Tagishsimon' from wikimedia commons)

Annie Lindsay, an archivist at the University Hospital London, said, 'it was the night sister's first duty to close the shutters and the day sister's duty to open them in the morning. If the shutters were not closed at night, then somebody unexpectedly died.'

Peter Fenwick, a neuropsychiatrist and an authority on the relationship between the mind and the brain at King's College London, says he cannot offer an observed explanation for stories of odd events and visions near the time of a death: 'They usually feature a deceased member of the family appearing to a dying person, helping them on a journey through physical death,' he says. 'People report that it is extremely pleasing. Occasionally, carers have reported seeing the vision, so it can't be down to hallucination due to medication. Where a patient is having a good death – by that I mean one with fewer painkillers – then these phenomena are more likely to occur.' Relatives and staff in hospices, including a doctor, have also reported seeing a room filled with light emanating from the body of a dying person. This is interpreted as 'the soul or the essence of the person' leaving the body.

Fenwick explains these phenomena:

As a neuroscientist, I have to say that when there is no brain activity, consciousness dies and you are gone. But the things that have been described to me might point to a continuation of consciousness. Who can say? Electricity was thought to be magic several hundred years ago. As we move to a postmodern view of science, together with the recognition that, as yet, neuroscience has no explanation for consciousness, the possibility of transcendent phenomena around the time of death should also be considered.

49a Museum Street, WC1

The Atlantis Bookshop is one of the world's oldest occult bookstores. Founded in 1922, it specialises in books on magic, ghosts and spiritualism and is haunted by a couple of presences, including its original owner. Many claim to have experienced a feeling of coldness before seeing a tall figure dressed in grey striding proudly and silently towards the back door before simply melting away.

The Atlantis has long been a hub for London's occult world. Gerald Gardner, a Wiccan and author, attended meetings of The Order of the Hidden Masters in its basement during his formative years, and the shop published his first book on witchcraft, the novel *High Magic's Aid*. It was here that he also met Ross Nichols, later a key figure in the Druid world, who edited Gardner's 1954 *Witchcraft Today*. So surely it would be expected that in a place such as this, surrounded by mystical and magical books, spells, potions and all things other worldly, that the odd spirit should pause before passing on its way.

The British Library, WC1

When the original library in Bloomsbury outgrew its space, a new one had to be constructed. A derelict goods yard in Euston Road near King's Cross station was the closet vacant site to the environs of the museum, where much of the library's collection of books and other materials was kept. It was also the only place in the locality capable of housing so many items, staff and services, and so it was to become the site of the 'new' library. Basements extend to a depth of 24.5m in this building spread over fourteen floors, nine of which are above ground, five below; 10 million bricks and

180,000 tonnes of concrete were needed to complete the building, which opened in 1999. If there are any spooks in the new facility no one is saying, but when building work was underway on this, the largest public building constructed in the UK in the twentieth century, builders reported the sound of 'unworldly' clanking chains during construction which always preceded the vision of the spirit of an eighteenth-century man. A civil servant saw a 'weeping man' according to a report in *The Sunday Times* of 19 May 1996. But why was this spectral figure weeping? No one seems to know.

Author's collection. (Gilly Pickup)

A Private Flat, Red Lion Square

Please note, the names used in the following tale have been changed. A strange story occurred in May 1971 when Jenny, staying in a spare room at her friend Harry's flat, was woken by another girl. The girl seemed very annoyed and asked Jenny why she was sleeping in her bed. Jenny apologised and explained that she had been invited to stay there for a couple of nights while she had some work done in her own flat. The girl said no more, left the room and Jenny fell asleep again. The following morning she mentioned the incident to Harry. He turned pale and explained that his flatmate who normally slept there was in hospital after a suicide attempt. They later discovered the girl, the vision who had spoken to Jenny, had died during the night.

More Than One Kind of Spirit

Going down the pub for the evening? You might get much more than you bargained for, besides a pint of Carlsberg and a packet of dry-roast peanuts. You could, if you are – umm – lucky, encounter a naughty poltergeist, hear phantom footsteps or see strange balls of light moving around. Okay, sometimes it may take several glasses of vino collapso before this starts to happen, but there are other times that you can have the strangest experiences, even if you don't touch a drop!

There are numerous public houses in London's West End where supernatural activity has been reported at some time or other. If you attribute hauntings to be a kind of 'recorded emotion' embedded upon the surroundings, it perhaps makes sense that public houses are more likely to be haunted than an average house. Just think of the emotions and numbers of people who have crossed their thresholds. Most common types of paranormal activity in pubs are noises and footsteps, though cases of 'cold spots' – pockets of numbingly cold air – and invisible 'nudgers' have also been reported.

But then, we probably all agree that surely no old public house steeped in history would be quite right without a resident spook.

Cock Tavern, Great Portland Street

Dating back to the late 1800s, the Cock Tavern is situated a stone's throw from the hustle and bustle of London's most famous shopping area, Oxford Street. Great Portland Street forms the boundary between Fitzrovia to the east and Marylebone to the west, and Charles Booth's map of 1889 shows Great Portland Street and the immediately parallel streets as 'middle-class' or 'well-to-do'. By comparison, though, accompanying notes describe it as a 'mixed street, shops, restaurants, many curio and antique shops, many doubtful massage establishments'.

The Cock Tavern. (Mike Pickup)

The Cock Tavern's spooky claim to fame is its cellar, haunted by some thing or things unknown. Although there have been no reported sightings, one landlord's dog got so freaked out about the cellar's mysterious guest that he simply refused to go down there. On other occasions, when customers remarked on a sudden icy chill which arrived suddenly and hung spookily in the air, the dog would growl and tentatively pad around something that no one else could see. Patrons have also reported vague shadows and wisps of ghostly cigar smoke which apparently come from nowhere. The reasons for these incidences are long since forgotten.

Ship Tavern, Gate Street off Kingsway
Established in 1549 at the height of the Reformation, the Ship Tavern has had plenty of time to acquire a good stock of ghosts. In its early days, it was half the size it is today and constructed mainly from timber. Originally, it was where exhausted labourers who were tending to the nearby fields – now partly Lincoln's Inn Fields – went to quench their thirst. It was also a favoured watering hole for some well-known folks of their day, people like shoemaker and antiquarian John Bagford and the Chevalier d'Eon, French diplomat and spy, who lived the first fifty years of her life as a man and the final thirty-two as a woman. Richard Penderell, who aided Charles II's escape, liked to pop into this pub to quaff his thirst too. Besides that, it was a secret meeting place for Catholics and there are those who declare that the ghosts of those executed nearby still return to meet here.

During the reign of Henry VIII, when Catholics were not allowed to practise

The Ship Tavern. (wikimedia common)

their faith, some would risk their lives to sneak into the Ship Tavern to attend Mass, which outlawed priests would conduct from behind the bar. A lookout would warn of imminent danger with a pre-arranged signal. This was to give priests time to escape into one of the pub's hidey holes, and the congregation would pick up their tankards and pretend there was nothing amiss. It was a jolly risky business though, because if they were discovered, their unfortunate fate was to be executed on the spot.

In 1780, this was the sad end for James Archer and his congregation, and his presence is believed to be one of those which haunt the pub. Staff complain of hearing things 'moving around' in the basement, while from time to time unearthly chilling screams have been heard in the dead of night. Sometimes a shadowy figure also creeps downstairs to the cellar – what chilling tales these walls could tell, if only they could speak.

Strangely, given the grim background of the Catholic hauntings, the pub also has a happy, mischievous prankster present that makes itself known by hiding cooking utensils or moving the cellar keys to other parts of the pub.

Private Chambers, Lincoln's Inn, Serle Street

While a student here in the 1800s, Robert Perceval, cousin of assassinated Prime Minister Spencer Perceval, was studying one evening in his room. As he pored over his books, the door opened silently and a shrouded figure entered. Terrified, Robert shouted at the presence, asking who it was and what its business was. There was no reply, so he picked up his sword and aimed it at the figure.

Lincoln's Inn. (Gilly Pickup)

Lincoln's Inn. (Mike Pickup)

The sword went right through it without seeming to cause it any harm. Robert lurched forward and pulled the cover from its head. He omitted a blood-curdling scream when he realised he was staring at an image of himself, blood pouring from open wounds on the doppelgänger's face. The spectre disappeared as abruptly as it had arrived. One day a few weeks later, his body was found lying in the street. He had been killed with his own sword and was battered around the areas where his double had bled.

Red Lion Square

Laid out in 1698, Red Lion Square marks the boundary between Holborn and Bloomsbury. Named for the Red Lion Inn that used to be on the site, the square is haunted by regicides Oliver Cromwell, John Bradshaw and Henry Ireton.

In 1649, after years of struggle between the authority of Parliament and the power of the king, Charles I was tried for high treason at Whitehall, found guilty and duly beheaded on a scaffold erected in front of the Banqueting House. He wore two shirts at his execution so he wouldn't shiver so much and would therefore appear less afraid.

He was replaced by Parliament, the coup led by Oliver Cromwell, John Bradshaw and Cromwell's son-in-law, Henry Ireton. The men were showered with lands and titles for their dedication to the cause of republicanism. However, their control was short-lived, because by 1661 all three had died and were buried in Westminster Abbey. Few Londoners were upset at the deaths of Cromwell and friends; after all, they'd closed theatres, inns, banned dancing and merriment, sports and make-up. Life under them was drab in the extreme.

It was a different story with Charles II. He liked a good party but when the time came for the Restoration of the monarchy, one of the first things he did was take revenge on the men who killed his father. Their remains were exhumed and some sources suggest that the bodies were brought to the Red Lion Inn. Other stories simply say that they were taken to Red Lion Square, where they were posthumously tried for regicide and found guilty. However, as Bradshaw's body had not been embalmed properly and had therefore decayed badly during the intervening years, the stench that emanated from it was disgusting.

After being exhumed they were unceremoniously hung on gallows at Tyburn all day before being beheaded. This was a symbolic execution marking the date of King Charles I's death in 1649. Their heads were displayed on spikes outside Westminster Hall as a deterrent to Parliamentarians who still opposed the king, and then their bodies were discarded in a pit, probably at Tyburn, though this is not clearly documented.

In the unsettling gloom of Red Lion Square, when night starts to cast unresolved shadows, you may just see the apparitions of the men as they walk and converse together before slowly fading away before your eyes.

Meanwhile, the spectre of John Bradshaw has also appeared several times in Westminster Abbey, perhaps regretting the loss of his exalted position. He was appointed President of the Commission at the trial of Charles I and was worried enough about his safety at the trial

Red Lion Square. (Gilly Pickup)

Westminster Abbey. (VisitBritain/Britain on View)

but having been sentenced to death he was not allowed to do so according to law and was removed from the court, soon to die at Whitehall.

Bradshaw used rooms at Westminster Abbey for his work after the trial and leased the deanery for a time. After his death in 1659 he was buried at the Abbey, until like the other regicides his body was dug up by the forces of Charles II. As befits such an ancient place with plenty of atmosphere, Bradshaw's ghost walks from the gallery he once used at the south-west of the Abbey and is reported to appear on the anniversary of Charles's death, 30 January.

Some Ghostly Snippets

to wear a bulletproof hat and a breast-plate. But unlike so many of those called to take part in the trial he did not shirk his responsibility; at the end of the trial, during which Charles refused to speak, Bradshaw read out an address justifying the trial and declared the King guilty. At that point, the King wished to speak,

- London is one of the world's most haunted cities
- 42 per cent of people claim to have experienced a supernatural encounter
- Spirits retain their personalities and can be helpful
- Ghosts may exist in a state of confusion and not have a clue what happened to them, why they are here, or why you cannot see or hear them

3

SOUTH

'Behind every man now alive stand 30 ghosts, for that is the ratio by which the dead outnumber the living.'
(Arthur C. Clarke, *2001: A Space Odyssey*)

50 Berkeley Square, Mayfair

Maggs Bros Ltd – isn't that a gloriously old-fashioned name for a shop? Since the 1930s, this Georgian townhouse in one of London's most elegant squares, one of the most prestigious addresses in the capital, has been home to these sellers of rare, antique and first-edition books. In 1998 the firm set the record for having the most expensive printed book, when it paid £4.2 million for a copy of the first book printed in England, William Caxton's *The Canterbury Tales*.

Oozing wealth and elegance, Berkeley Square has long been home of the rich and famous. It is one of those streets where titles and butlers are par for the course. Winston Churchill lived at No. 48 as a child, Horace Walpole, son of Prime Minister Robert Walpole, lived at No. 11 during the 1700s, and Robert Clive of India bought No. 45 in 1761 and committed suicide there in 1774.

The fictional Bertie Wooster and his valet Jeeves, creations of author P.G. Wodehouse, also lived in the square which was even posh enough for Charles Rolls (of Rolls-Royce fame) to be born there.

Before Maggs Bros took over at No. 50 Berkeley Square, the house was the home of former Prime Minister George Canning until he died in 1827. It then

Maggs Bros, Berkeley Square.
(VisitLondon images/Britain on View)

Berkeley Square. (Gilly Pickup)

belonged to a Miss Curzon until she died aged around 90 years old in 1859. So far, so quaint. But, of course, there is a more sinister side to this story, and as you will see there are good reasons for this to be called London's most haunted house.

'It seems that a Something or Other, very terrible indeed, haunts or did haunt a particular room. This unnamed Raw Head and Bloody Bones, or whatever it is, has been sufficiently awful to have caused the death, in convulsions, of at least two foolhardy persons who have dared to sleep in that chamber …' so said Charles Harper in his book *Haunted Houses* (1907).

Some reports say that George Canning claimed to have heard strange noises and experienced psychic phenomena whilst living there, but there is no record of anything untoward happening during Miss Curzon's residency. It was not until after her death that the house gained a full-blown reputation for being seriously spooky.

Many stories relate to paranormal activity being at its busiest in the rooms on the top floor. Theories have been bandied about as to the reasons for these

happenings, but all we can do is piece together the fragments of anecdotes – after all, few who encountered the horrors of the house lived to tell the tale, and those who did survive were always left insane.

A man called Myers rented the building in the late 1800s. His fiancée called off their engagement and, broken-hearted, he became a recluse, hardly venturing from a room at the top of the house. After he died, two people were said to have died of fright after staying in the same room, while another said Mr Myer's ghost chased him from the house.

Another story concerns a Mr Dupre who once lived here and kept his insane brother locked in a room on the top floor. The brother was supposedly so violent that he had to be fed through an opening in the door. His groans could be heard in neighbouring houses and it is thought that after he died, he became a horrific white-faced spectre with a gaping jaw, which terrified the wits out of anyone who saw him at a window. Other reports tell of an attic room that is haunted by a young woman called Adeline who threw herself out of the window to escape an abusive uncle. Yet another rumour is that a little girl was murdered in the top-floor nursery. Her ghost has been seen wringing her hands in despair and sobbing.

But, as we all know, stories like this tend to become enhanced and embroidered over time and some specific incidents may well be over-fertile imaginations. We must remember that in the early nineteenth century, few poor and working-class Londoners could read and write. News which travelled by word of mouth was often misstated and exaggerated, and as stories passed from person to person, reports about ghostly goings-on would have become distorted and mixed up.

However, there is a well-documented story concerning a maid who was employed to work in the house in the 1800s. On her first night in the attic room, she woke the whole household with a piercing scream. Rushing in, they found her in a state of shock, shaking from head to foot, and when they asked what the matter was, she could only describe what she saw as 'so horrible' before lapsing into unconsciousness. The following day she died without regaining consciousness in St George's Hospital.

Another tale of death associated with one of the rooms on the top floor is that of 30-year-old Sir Robert Warboys. His friend, Lord Cholmondley, had introduced him to John Benson who, at that time in the mid-1800s, owned 50 Berkeley Square. One evening, over brandy and cigars, the subject turned to the hauntings in the house. Sir Robert threw his head back and laughed – 'Utter nonsense! There is no such thing as ghosts.' The other two set a wager of 100 guineas, saying that he would not be able to spend a night in the haunted

room. Sir Robert accepted immediately. However, there must have been a degree of bravado there and he couldn't have been enitrely comfortable as he took a bell to bed with him to raise the alarm if he saw or heard anything unusual. He also carried a pistol for further protection. A short while later, his companions heard the bell's frantic ring followed by three shots. They ran to the room to encounter a terrible sight. Sir Robert was dead, his face set in an expression of sheer terror. The odd thing was, there was no sign of a gunshot wound or bullets.

We know of at least one survivor of the evils of the top floor. He was rake, serial seducer and a Member of Parliament, Thomas Lyttelton (1744–1779). Armed with two blunderbusses loaded with silver coins (believed to combat evil), he is said to have shot a 'thing' during the night and saw it fall, though no evidence of anything was visible the following day. Lord Lyttelton was quoted as saying, 'it is quite true that there is a house in Berkeley Square (No. 50), said to be haunted, and long unoccupied on that account. There are strange stories about it, into which this deponent cannot enter.'

Interestingly, Lyttelton, who had a house nearby in Hill Street, also had a prophetic dream on 24 November 1779. In the dream he saw a wraith which told him he would die within three days. He was so frightened that when he woke up, he called for a servant who discovered his master lying in bed 'shaking and sweating'. He decided to leave London and travel to his mansion in Epsom where, as prophesied, he died of a fit on 27 November 1779.

In the days before his death and following the dream, he mentioned it to friends Rowan Hamilton and Captain Ascough. It was passed on, in the way these stories are, to another lady named Mrs Thrale, who wrote it in her diary on Sunday, 28 November, the morning after Lyttelton's death. She said:

Yesterday a lady from Wales dropped in and said that she had been at Drury Lane on Friday night. 'How,' I asked, 'were you entertained?' 'Very strangely indeed! Not with the play, though, but the discourse of a Captain Ascough, who averred that a friend of his, Lord Lyttelton, has seen a spirit, who warned him that he will die in three days. I have thought of nothing else since.

Back to 50 Berkeley Square: in his book *Phantoms of the Night* (1956), Elliot O' Donnell tells the story of Edward Blunden and Robert Martin, two sailors from HMS *Penelope*, who arrived in London from the West Indies on Christmas Eve 1887. Desperate for somewhere to stay but having squandered all their money on drink, they came upon the empty building of 50 Berkeley Square. They managed to break in but found the downstairs rooms too damp to sleep in, so went upstairs. Not long afterwards they heard the sound of heavy footsteps ascending the staircase. Then something, described as 'a hideous, shapeless mass', burst into the room, filling it from floor to ceiling. Petrified and ignoring the screams of his companion, Martin threw himself downstairs and outside, straight into the arms of a passing policeman. In the meantime, Blunden, who was trapped in the room with the 'thing', jumped from a window. His body was impaled on a spiked railing bordering the pavement at the front of the house, his face twisted in agony, eyes bulging from their sockets.

It was as if all Hell had let loose inside this house ... had the Powers of Darkness taken over?

Jessie Adelaide Middleton's *Grey Ghost Book* (Nash & Grayson, 1930) tells us:

The mystery of Berkeley Square still remains. The story of the haunted house in Mayfair can be recapitulated in a few words; the house contains at least one room of which the atmosphere is supernaturally fatal to body and mind. A girl saw, heard and felt such horror in it that she went mad, and never recovered sanity enough to tell how or why. A gentleman, a disbeliever in ghosts, dared to sleep in number 50 and was found a corpse in the middle of the floor after frantically ringing for help in vain. Rumour suggests other cases of the same kind, all ending in death, madness, or both as a result of sleeping, or trying to sleep in that room.

Certainly sounds bloodcurdling ... she goes on to say:

The very party walls of the house, when touched, are found saturated with electric horror. It is uninhabited save by an elderly man and his wife who act as caretakers; but even these have no access to the room. This is kept locked, the key being in the hands of a mysterious and seemingly nameless person who comes to the house once every six months, locks up the elderly couple in the basement, and then unlocks the room and occupies himself in it for hours.

Other bizarre happenings associated with the house include sounds of furniture being dragged across the floor, bells ringing, lights flashing on and off, pain-racked screams coming from behind locked doors, windows banging, items being thrown on to the street and figures dressed in period costume peering from the windows. While paranormal activity seems to have slowed in recent years, a police notice from the 1950s still hangs on the wall warning people not to ascend to the top floor.

According to Charles Harper's book *Haunted Houses* (1907),

> The haunted house in Berkeley Square was long one of those things that no country cousin come up from the provinces to London on sightseeing bent, ever willingly missed. But truth to tell, its exterior is now a trifle disappointing to the casual seeker after horrors. Viewed in the afternoon sunshine with a milkman delivering the usual half pint, or quart, as the case may be, is just as respectably commonplace as any other house of similar late Georgian period, and even at the weird stroke of 12, when the midnight policeman comes and thrusts a burly shoulder against the front-door, and tries the area-gate or flashes a gleam over the kitchen windows from his bulls-eye, there is nothing at all hair-raising about it.

Harper continues:

> There was a time when number 50 wore an exceedingly uncared for appearance. Soap, paint and whitewash were unused for years, and grime clung to brickwork and windows alike. The area was choked with wasted hand-bills, wisps of straw, and all the accumulations that speedily made a derelict London house. The very

picture of misery; and every passing stranger stopped the first errand-boy, and asked various questions, to which the answer was, generally, 'aunted 'ouse.

In January 1937, a Mrs Mary Balfour moved into a flat in Charles Street, adjacent to Berkeley Square. One night, in a state of agitation her maid asked if she would come to the kitchen, which was at the back of the flat, as she said she had seen something strange from the window. The maid drew Mrs Balfour's attention to one of the windows of 50 Berkeley Square, where a man stood dressed in a silver-coloured coat and breeches. He wore a periwig and his face was ashen. The women decided he must have been to a fancy dress party, because of the way he was dressed. It was not until a couple of weeks later that Mrs Balfour and her maid learned from a doctor that they had sighted one of the spectres of 50 Berkeley Square.

50 Berkeley Square. (Mike Pickup)

Maybe it's all well and good to think that the ghoulish tales surrounding 50 Berkeley Square come from a time long gone and don't apply to this day and age. Perhaps, however, the spectral shenanigans in that house have not yet been stilled – in 2001 a young woman working in the bookshop on a Saturday morning said she witnessed a mass of brown mist. It moved speedily across the room before vanishing. That same year, a cleaning lady felt the presence of someone standing behind her, but when she turned round there was nobody there; and on one occasion, a man walking up the staircase suddenly had his glasses snatched from his hand and flung to the floor.

Is it purely overactive imaginations, or is it truly ghoulish presences that continue to haunt 50 Berkeley Square? Would you stay the night alone in one of the top floor rooms?

44 Berkeley Square

Close to the chilling 50 Berkeley Square is another elegant property, one which features in the strange tale of one of the twentieth century's most baffling and still unexplained mysteries – Lord Lucan's disappearance. On November 7 1974, his children's nanny was found dead in their house in Lower Belgrave Street. She had been brutally murdered. His Lordship disappeared, never to be seen again, so giving rise to the belief that he was the murderer. Before he vanished, he spent much of his free time at the casino tables at the Clermont Club at 44 Berkeley Square. In fact, in 1960, after winning more than £26,000, he decided to devote himself full-time to gambling.

Not that the resident phantom is that of the elusive peer himself; indeed, no one knows whether the aristocrat and professional gambler is in fact alive or dead.

Nikolaus Pevsner described 44 Berkeley Square as 'the finest terrace house of London' (perhaps rather an over-generalisation), whilst Horace Walpole, a frequent visitor, applauded the building's staircase as being 'as beautiful a piece of scenery and, considering the space, of art as can be imagined'. It is undoubtedly a magnificent staircase, designed in 1742 by William Kent for Lady Isabella Finch, a Maid of Honour to George II's sister, Princess Amelia. She regularly entertained luminaries of her age, while her loyal major-domo, a dashing figure in green livery and powdered wig, watched over the proceedings and made sure the servants did as they were told.

In later times, the house was purchased by Lord Clermont, who frequently entertained the Prince Regent who would become George IV, and after a succession of owners, the Clermont Club took occupancy in 1959. It seems that it is Lady Finch's major-domo who continues to linger on in spirit form, and over the last 200 years, his presence has been seen as it flits up and down the grand staircase, keeping a watchful eye on those who play roulette and backgammon in the grand salon. He walks with a slight limp and his appearances are brief. It is as though after having satisfied himself that all is well, he simply melts through one of the doors and ascends the narrow, spiral staircase to his bedroom at the top of the house.

52/53 Berkeley Square

In the early 1900s on moonlit nights, the sad figure of a bewigged man dressed in a satin coat, finished with lace, could be seen looking out of the first-floor window of this house, overlooking the square. Those who saw him said he was wringing his hands and had a hopeless expression on his face.

In the eighteenth century, a middle-aged man lived here with his daughter. After a few years she eloped, but out of love for her father she promised she would return after her wedding. The father waited patiently for her arrival but died of a broken heart when she did not return to her former home. If you are passing this building on Berkeley Square on a late chill afternoon just as twilight drapes itself across the streets, take time to pause and look up at the window. You may just see the poignant phantom looking longingly with mournful eyes for his daughter to return.

An interesting fact: Berkeley Square is where London's oldest plane trees were planted by Edward Bouverie who lived at No. 13. The tree opposite Berkeley House is London's highest valued tree, estimated to be worth a monumental £750,000 in 2008.

St James's Park

Following the Restoration of the monarchy, the jovial King Charles II decided to make major changes to St James's Park. His inspiration was drawn from gardens of French palaces he had seen while he was in exile. He ordered the redesign which included the laying of lawns and planting avenues of trees. He decided that this once swampy wasteland should have a magnificent centrepiece too – a 2,560ft long, 125ft wide canal, lined on each side with trees. After it was finished, the new park was opened to the public for the first time. King Charles II entertained guests here and this was where he often courted his favourite mistress, Nell Gwyn. The diarist, John Evelyn, a contemporary of Samuel Pepys, wrote on 4 March 1671: 'I had a faire opportunity of talking to his Majestie ... & thence walked with him thro St. James's Parke to the Garden, where I both saw and heard a very familiar discourse between ... [the King] & Mrs. Nellie.'

However, the park also gained rather an unsavoury reputation. The poet Rochester describes the park in the decade after the Restoration: 'Carmen, divines, great lords, and tailors, / Prentices, poets, pimps, and jailers, / Footmen, fine fops do here arrive, / And here promiscuously they swive.'

Things hadn't improved much by 1759, when one James Brown admitted to blackmailing 500 or more men there after he had picked them up in Birdcage Alley. He was sentenced at the Old Bailey to be hanged for robbery.

Even a century later, it still wasn't one of the best places to go after dark. A reader under the pen-name 'a Pedestrian' wrote to the *Daily Telegraph* in 1855 and said of the park: 'I am constantly annoyed by prostitutes.' He was in the habit of cutting through St James's Park and Green Park on his way from Westminster to Piccadilly. 'As soon as it becomes dusk, they will not let anybody pass without attempting to detain them. I have complained to the police until I am tired of doing so, the only answer I ever get being, "Then you should go another way".'

But to have a gander at the origin of the ghoul in this anecdote, we have to go back to the eighteenth century when Horse Guards Parade was created after part of the canal was filled in. Soon after that, the rest of the canal was turned into a lake which has a somewhat gruesome story attached to it.

At the end of that century, a sergeant – or according to some versions an officer – in the Coldstream Guards (the oldest regiment in the Army) murdered his wife. After she was dead, he cut her head off, and as he was dumping her body in the lake another soldier saw him.

There is no record of what happened to the murderer but since then there have been regular sightings of the woman's ghost in this, London's oldest royal park. Known as the 'Red Lady', sometimes she walks from the Cockpit Steps – so called because it was once the site of the Royal Cockpit – towards the lake; at other times she rises eerily from the water. Some say she wears a 'red striped' dress, though others who have seen her say she wears a pale-coloured dress covered in blood. Sometimes blood gushes from her neck, and people have reported the sickly smell of fresh blood when she appears. Sometimes she is seen beckoning to visitors as she appears from the water.

There used to be a barracks in the park, and the Red Lady once terrified the life out of two soldiers on guard there, according to *The Times* in January 1804. In fact, they were so petrified that they were unfit to return to duty for a considerable time. One source suggests that the soldiers, Privates George Jones and Richard Donkin of the Coldstream Guards, encountered the phantom separately and independently, though descriptions from both were similar.

Stuff and nonsense? Well, in 1972 a car driver who veered off the road nearby was acquitted of dangerous driving when the horrible apparition was cited as cause. Interestingly, the legal establishment obviously accepted the spectre's existence.

St James's Palace, Pall Mall

As the home and offices for several members of the Royal Family, St James's Palace, with its long and much splendid history, is also where official functions are held. But when you add in a healthy dose of mysterious happenings from days of yore, it is not surprising that it houses a hair-raising spectre.

Much survives of the original red-brick building, including turrets, two surviving Tudor rooms in the State apartments and the Chapel Royal. This is where, in September 1997, Princess Diana's coffin was kept for a few days before being taken to Kensington Palace on the eve of her funeral at Westminster Abbey. The great Tudor Gatehouse at the southern end of St James's Street still stands strong too. It bears Henry VIII's royal cipher 'HR' surmounted by his crown, above the original foot passages leading through to Colour Court.

The palace was commissioned by Henry VIII on the site of a former leper hospital. In the following years, two of Henry's children – Henry FitzRoy, 1st Duke of Richmond and Somerset, and Mary I – died here. The heart and bowels of the latter were buried in the palace's Chapel Royal. Charles I slept here once, rather fitfully one would imagine, as it was his final night before his execution. Queen Anne was born here in 1665 and nearly all of her seventeen children were born here too, though sadly none survived.

But it seems that the spectre comes from a later time. On the night of 30/31 May 1810, the arrogant Ernest Augustus, Duke of Cumberland and fifth son of King George III, returned to his rooms late after an evening at the opera. What happened next is open to speculation, but it ended with the death of the Duke's valet, Joseph Sellis, whose throat was cut so savagely that his head was almost severed from his body. The Duke claimed Sellis tried to assassinate him but ran off after he fought back and, aghast at what he had done, committed suicide. The London public, however, preferred to think the unpopular Duke had murdered his valet. Stories say that the Duke was being blackmailed because he got the poor servant's daughter pregnant and that she committed suicide rather than live with the shame. Rumours were hardly quelled by serious inadequacies with the Duke's testimony. However, as was the way with some aristocratic toffs in those days, the Duke literally got away with murder.

His valet's gruesome apparition still haunts the Palace, lying on top of blood-drenched sheets with his jaw hanging open, his head still joined to his body only by a sliver, a terrible silent scream etched on his face.

A House in St James's Place

In the 1800s, two unmarried sisters, Ann and Harriet Pearson, lived together in an old rambling house in St James's Place. After Ann died in 1858, Harriet lived in the house alone. In November 1864, while on a visit to Brighton, she became ill and was brought back to her London home to be nursed by her housekeeper Eliza Quintin. Two nieces, Mrs Coppinger and Miss Emma Pearson, as well as her nephew's wife, Mrs John Pearson, were also staying in the house at the time.

It was on 23 December, a chill evening with a thick London peasouper swirling around that the strangest thing happened. The others had gone to bed after taking turns to sit with Harriet, leaving Mrs Pearson to look after their ill aunt. They all left their doors open and the landing light burning. At about one in the morning Mrs Coppinger and Miss Pearson jerked awake and saw their dead Aunt Ann go past the door and into the sick room. At the same time, Mrs Pearson ran into their room, in a state of agitation and fear. She too had seen and recognised the dead woman. All three immediately went to their aunt's bedside. She was sitting upright and told them that she had just seen her sister. 'I know Ann has come to take me away on my final journey,' she told them calmly. Shortly afterwards, Harriet fell into a coma and passed away at 6 o'clock that evening.

More Theatrical Ghosts

Her Majesty's Theatre, Haymarket
Although Andrew Lloyd Webber's long running *Phantom of the Opera* plays in Her Majesty's Theatre, it is not the only phantom associated with this theatre. Constructed in 1897 for Royal Academy of Dramatic Art (RADA) founder and actor-manager Sir Beerbohm Tree, it is said that he often comes back to haunt the building. In his lifetime, he liked to watch performances from the top box

Her Majesty's Theatre. (Mike Pickup)

stage right, and this is the centre for manifestations reported today. Occupants sometimes complain of cold spots and say that occasionally, the door to the box suddenly opens slowly of its own accord as if allowing access to someone, though this someone is invisible.

Not that the ghost of Sir Beerbohm restricts his activities to this area. In 1978, during a performance of *Cause Celebre*, the cast of the play, including actress Glynis Johns, saw a spectral figure glide across the theatre at the back of the stalls and disappear. There was no doubt in the minds of those who saw him that it was Sir Beerbohm. There are also rumours that legendary comedian Tommy Cooper still wanders around Her Majesty's Theatre after his death on stage here in 1984.

Phantom of the Opera at Her Majesty's Theatre, Haymarket. (westendmediacentre.com)

Her Majesty's Theatre. (Mike Pickup)

Piccadilly Theatre, Denman Street

On 27 April 1928, the Piccadilly Theatre opened with a musical play called *Blue Eyes*. Evelyn Laye, known as 'Boo' to her friends, a nickname she was given as a child, was in the starring role. This beautiful actress who had a glittering career is quite possibly the West End's most modern spirit as she only died in 1996. Although not well remembered now, she was a big star of her day, and one of her great fans was King George VI. Her picture hangs in the theatre office, and it was when it was removed that poltergeist activity began. It seemed that Evelyn, or the poltergeist, wanted her picture to stay where it was. In fact, the poltergeist grew furious, tossing papers, books, folders and office items here, there and everywhere. Piles of stationary would slide unaccountably from shelves; even bottles of ink would fly around the room. When the picture was returned to the office wall, the supernatural activity calmed down again.

Victoria Palace Theatre, Victoria Street

Less sinister is the poltergeist in the Victoria Palace Theatre, a handsome building with a grey marble foyer adorned with gold mosaic and white Sicilian marble pillars. This naughty manifestation likes to give guests a hair-rising experience – literally. This presence obviously has a fetish for wigs as when it frequents the corridors,

Victoria Palace Theatre. (wikimedia commons)

hairpieces have been reported to fly through the air for no apparent reason. There have also been reports of locked doors opening and closing of their own accord. Watch out if you visit the Victoria Palace and your hair is not your own – cheeky poltergeist!

Queen's Theatre, Shaftesbury Avenue

Another light-hearted spirit haunts the Queen's Theatre. In 1913, the Queen's was popular for its 'tango teas', which cost 2s and 6d for dancing and tea, and there is just a chance that this naughty spirit comes from this time. Male members of staff who work here have had feelings of being ogled as they change into their uniforms before a performance. There have also been reports that some of them have had their bottoms pinched by an invisible presence. Ooh yes, really!

Garrick Theatre, Charing Cross Road

Arthur Bourchier managed several West End theatres during his career, including the Royalty, the Criterion, His Majesty's (renamed as Her Majesty's Theatre in 1952) and the Strand (now known as the Novello). He managed the Garrick Theatre for fifteen years, longer than any of the others, which is presumably why he chooses to haunt this one. Known for his dislike of critics, he refused entry to the drama critic of *The Times* in 1913. Arthur often appears on the rear stairway just after a performance, or makes his presence known and scares people out of their wits by tapping them on their backs. During a refurbishment a few years ago, Arthur appeared large-as-life in front of amazed workmen in the upper balcony. But please don't worry if you are slightly nervous at the possible

Garrick Theatre. (VisitLondon images/Britain on View/Pawel Libera)

prospect of bumping into a ghostly Arthur. If you have come to see a show, it is unlikely you will spot him as he usually only materialises to actors and others who work in the theatre.

Lyric Theatre, Shaftesbury Avenue

The Lyric Theatre, in Shaftesbury Avenue, is where the ghost of Nellie Klute, a programme seller and usherette, returns occasionally to watch shows. She has been seen walking down an aisle, although her favourite spot, when she is not watching a show, is front of house. During a séance in the theatre in 1972, a medium contacted Nellie, who he said spoke to him in a whisper. It seems a jealous lover murdered her there in the early twentieth century. According to two theatregoers, Emily and Fred Burnes, 'a lady dressed in old fashioned clothes' tried to sell them a programme when they arrived at the theatre to see *Irma La Douce* in 1958. 'She seemed strange, nervous,' they reported. 'When she began to disappear before our eyes we thought we were going mad.' However, although there were other patrons in the foyer at the time, no one else seemed to be aware of the phantom programme seller. Those who have sensed her presence say it is preceded by a sound like paper rustling.

And Now For Another Creepy Crowd of Pub Spirits

Share a drink with a publican and it is very possible they will tell you of a few dark secrets embedded within the walls of their drinking hole. Read on for some more West End pubs bristling with ghostly goings-on – which you can believe or not, as you will.

John Snow Public House, Soho

This Soho pub with thick and mullioned windows is named after a doctor, the first to understand that contaminated water was the reason for outbreaks of cholera. In 1854, he tracked the source of one particularly devastating Soho outbreak to a pump in Broad Street (now Broadwick Street). 'He who drinks a tumbler of London water has literally in his stomach more animated beings than there are men, women and children on the face of the globe', wrote clergymen Sydney Smith in a letter to a friend, and in those days, he was not far wrong.

The pub, originally called the Newcastle-upon-Tyne, was renamed in Dr Snow's honour and built on the site

Lyric Theatre. (wikipedia)

John Snow Pub, Soho. (wikimedia commons)

of his surgery, which in its day teemed with the wretched and dying, and which probably accounts for the wraith-like figure, more of which in a minute. John Snow, incidentally, was one of the first surgeons to use anaesthetics, and gave Queen Victoria chloroform in 1853 for Prince Leopold's birth.

In 1854, in a letter to the editor of the *Medical Times and Gazette*, Snow wrote:

On proceeding to the spot, I found that nearly all the deaths had taken place within a short distance of the [Broad Street] pump. With regard to the deaths occurring in the locality belonging to the pump, there were 61 instances in which I was informed that the deceased persons used to drink the pump water from Broad Street. The result of the inquiry is that there has been no particular outbreak or prevalence of cholera in this part of London except among the persons who were in the habit of drinking the water of the above-mentioned pump well.

Later researchers discovered that this public well was only 3ft from an old cesspit, which leaked faecal bacteria. The nappies of a baby who had contracted cholera were washed in this cesspit. It was common at the time to have a cesspit under most homes. Most families tried to have their raw sewage collected and dumped in the Thames to prevent their cesspit from filling faster than sewage could decompose into the soil.

Patrons have witnessed the spectre of an unknown man sitting on a corner seat in this pub. A woman who saw him twice said an 'intense feeling' precedes his appearance. Others have described the phantom as 'a pathetic figure with red, watery eyes. He looks as if he is in pain.' Some of those who see it have mistaken the spectre for a real person, at least until the moment it rises from its seat and passes right through them. The ghoul is suspected to be a cholera victim. One pub manager said that sometimes when working alone in his office, he felt someone walk into the room. When he turned round to see who it was, no one was there.

Whoever this phantom was in life, one thing is for certain – it is not John Snow. He didn't drink and was a member of the Temperance Society.

Silver Cross, Whitehall

A sixteenth-century law, which has never been repealed, means the Silver Cross pub near Trafalgar Square is still an officially licensed brothel. Old maps show that it is located directly opposite the site where Oliver Cromwell's house once stood. There have been countless strange occurrences and sightings here, believed to be the spirits of former prostitutes, including one who was murdered in what is now the lounge of the pub. Spooky happenings include cold sensations, strange noises, fingers scratching and tapping at doors, and pictures randomly falling off walls. On several occasions in 1997, the landlady reported hearing a spectral female voice crying out 'Daniel' in the middle of the night. All the more chilling, as that was the name of her own son. Others also heard the voice and it continued for several months before stopping as abruptly as it began.

The George, the Strand

From the twelfth century onwards, grand palaces and townhouses lined the Strand. The nobility, bishops and royal courtiers inhabited these, and many had their own river gates and landings directly on the Thames. Essex House was one such grand home. It was built around 1757 for Robert Dudley, Earl of Leicester, and was originally called Leicester House but was renamed Essex House after being inherited by Robert Devereux, 2nd Earl of Essex, in 1588. There was Arundel House too, home to the Howards, the Earls of Arundel. Demolished in 1678, Arundel Street, adjoining the Strand, was built on the site of the house. Other homes which belonged to these fine and fancy folk included Somerset House, built by Edward Seymour, the Duke of Somerset, Regent of England from 1547–49, and Savoy Palace, London, home of John of Gaunt, King Richard II's uncle. In the fourteenth century, the Savoy was the most magnificent nobleman's mansion in England. Today, the Savoy Hotel stands on the site. Worcester House, the Bishop of Carlisle's home, Salisbury House, Durham House and York House, home of the Dukes of Buckingham, all stood here too.

Although the black and white timbered frontage of The George only dates from the 1930s, this public house, characterised by bare floorboards and open fires in winter, is built on much older foundations. Originally founded in 1723 as a coffee house, it is not clear whether it was named after the reigning monarch, George III, or its original proprietor, a man called George Simpkins. It became George's Hotel in 1830 but whoever it was named for, the picture on the pub sign is that of George III.

There is a long tradition of a handsome phantom appearing to startled witnesses in the cellar of the George. One of those documented occurred during a refurbishment in the 1970s. Painters and decorators arrived one morning to start work and, having allotted various tasks to his men, the foreman went down into the cellar and started whitewashing the walls. A short while later he came racing back upstairs, white-faced and trembling. 'That feller down there gu'vnor,' he said to the landlord, 'he just looked at me, didn't

say nothin', just stared.' The landlord calmed him down with a glass of brandy and then asked him what the man had looked like. 'All 'istorical like them Roundheads and Cavaliers,' came the breathless reply. The landlord nodded. 'Oh I shouldn't worry about him,' he reassured the unfortunate workman. 'That's just the ghost. My wife sees him all the time.' Quite who he is, or was, nobody has been able to ascertain, but he is almost certainly a nobleman who lived in the Strand in days of old.

The Morpeth Arms, Millbank

Millbank Prison opened in 1816 and closed in 1890. For part of its history, it served as a holding facility for convicted prisoners before they were transported to Australia. Conditions in the prison were harsh, with over a thousand prisoners incarcerated in tiny spaces, so many were unable even to stand up. The Tate Gallery was built on the site of the prison while the pub, which dates back to 1845, stands on part of the prison grounds.

The cells beneath the Morpeth Arms house at least a couple of spooky inhabitants; one is the troubled spirit of a convict who died before he was sent to Australia. Some say he committed suicide rather than be sent to the other side of the world. When daylight bleeds away, it is not surprising that staff have a reluctance to enter the gloomy cellars because of the oppressive atmosphere. A shady figure also materialises there occasionally. Sounds of scratching and scrabbling have been heard, possibly the ghosts of starving, disease-ridden prisoners who were driven almost mad while awaiting their fate. Strange happenings have been reported in the pub, including incidents where customers have had their drinks knocked out of their hands by an invisible presence, and bottles which inexplicably fall to the floor when no one is near.

Moving Away from the Pub

Naval and Military Club, 94 Piccadilly Cambridge House is a Grade I Listed Palladian-style building, dating from 1761. Throughout its history, it has been associated with many notable people, but it was during its time as the Naval and Military Club that it gained its reputation of being haunted by a Second World War serviceman. The Club was popularly known as the 'In & Out Club' due to the words on the gateposts.

On 21 April 1994, an article by John Darnton appeared in the New York edition of *The New York Times*. The article, 'a Blessed Haunted Plot, This England', told of the sighting of a ghost at the Naval and Military Club:

> Trevor Newton, the white-haired, 52-year-old night porter at the Naval and Military Club, seems a solid, feet-on-the-ground type. But try telling him that there's no such thing as a ghost, and his eyes widen so that his visage is transformed into a sepulchral mask and he leans forward to lower his voice conspiratorially: 'If anyone had said to me there's such a thing – never, no way would I have believed it. But I know what I saw. I saw it, and it was frightening'.

Mr Newton's position on the supernatural changed on Tuesday, 15 March at 3.07 a.m., when he was making his rounds on the club's second floor. He entered the vaulted Egremont Room, somewhat surprised that the outdoor balcony lights were on, casting their eerie glow through the 20ft-tall windows. He walked to the fireplace, punched his timecard in a slot in the wall and turned around.

'It was then I saw it,' he said. 'About six foot tall. White hair swept back, brown coat. I can't recollect any face whatsoever. It moved over toward the wall. I froze for a second. Then I got out of there – quick, to be honest. It was all over in a matter of seconds.'

Everyone seemed to agree that the aging Naval and Military Club on Piccadilly was the perfect venue for a sighting. It has two burning torches along the front wall; a lobby with red-topped leather writing desks; canvasses of gory war scenes crammed with raised sabres, dying horses and cannon smoke; a silver gong from a German destroyer scuttled in 1918, and entombed in a glass case and brown with age, the epaulettes worn by Lieutenant Colonel E.J. Watson, 59th Bengal Native Infantry, retired 1853.

By dint of the quick-fire spreading of news and some rapid deduction – Mr Newton told 34-year-old Mark Brabbs, an assistant steward, who telephoned his father, Peter Brabbs, who had worked at the club for fifty years before his retirement – the apparition was identified. The key was the swept-back hair and the Second World War ankle-length brown trench coat. It was Major William Henry Braddell, known as 'Perky' because of his cheerful demeanour.

Major Braddell had served with the Royal Dublin Fusiliers in France, and was shot in the knee at Somme before being captured and incarcerated for four years by the Germans. 'He was true to and maintained the highest traditions of his regiment,' brother officers recalled.

He was last seen at the club in the Egremont Room on 5 May 1940. He was preparing to dine there with two friends, Colonel William Gordon and one Major Crozier, when he was summoned for a telephone call downstairs. A bomb struck the room while he was away. Returning to find his friends dead, he was reported to have remarked, 'What a dreadful business.'

A little over a week later, while commanding an anti-aircraft battery in Kensington, he too was caught in a German air raid and killed. His obituary did not give his age, but it is thought that he was in his early 50s. Once the apparition had a name and the name appeared in the newspapers, the oldest among the club's 3,500 members tried to put a face to it. Not many could place him, but Brigadier J.R. Fishbourne wrote in to say that he served under Perky as a subaltern. He recalled the trench coat and added, 'I don't remember much else about him except that he was quite a keen bridge player, and I think his favourite occasional tipple was sherry and bitters.'

Commander Anthony Holt, the club's secretary, said he felt that it was natural that, if the major's ghost should appear anywhere, it would be at the club: 'It's because it's the place he thought of most as home. We pride ourselves on looking after the members. They become attached.'

Legend has it that at least one other spirit frequents the club. Some visitors looking at a portrait of Lord Nelson standing oddly off-centre swear they have seen the image of his mistress, Emma Hamilton, glowing out of a dark patch beside him. Others report a whooshing sound and a sudden draft in the Octagonal Room, where Lord Palmerston charted the nation's course as prime minister in the mid-1800s, and where an officer committed suicide by leaping from an open window.

Some believe they have encountered Lady Caroline Lamb, the beautiful and impulsive wife of Lord Melbourne, who fell in love with Lord Byron. She died, it is said, by striking her head upon a mantelpiece. 'Did she fall or was she pushed?' Commander Holt said, 'No one knows. I've had a detailed letter from a member recounting an instance in 1958 when he stayed here. He awoke in the middle of the night to find a woman sitting on the end of his bed. He spoke to her – he thought she was his wife – and she didn't answer. Then he realised his wife was fast asleep beside him.'

The Commander is convinced that if the mostly recently sighted apparition does indeed belong to Major Braddell, then it is unlikely to be malevolent. He has said as much to Mr Newton, but the night porter is beyond convincing. He shook his head and said, 'I don't mind telling you, I feel uneasy every night I come.'

Accounts of the manifestation also appeared in British papers: The *Evening Standard* on 11 March and *The Times* on 15 March 1994.

Golden Square, Soho

In 1665 an outbreak of Bubonic Plague rampaged across London. Before long, thousands had died and the pits, dug to receive the bodies, were full. The plague was a horrific way to die. The victim's skin turned black in patches and inflamed glands or 'buboes' in the groin, combined with compulsive vomiting, a swollen tongue and splitting headaches made it an agonising killer. At night, corpses were brought out in answer to the cry of 'Bring out your dead', and were piled into a cart and taken away to the plague pits.

London plague pits have attracted more than their fair share of ghoulish stories. No wonder, when you consider that during the plague many sufferers were tossed into the pit while they were still alive. There is a legend which tells if you walk past the site of the pit in Charterhouse Square late at night, the screams and wails of these poor people can still be heard.

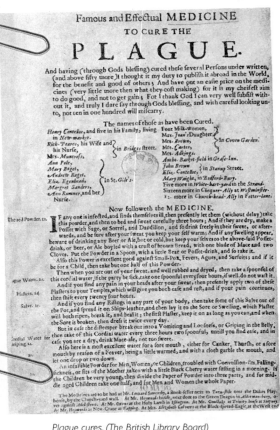

Plague cures. (The British Library Board)

During the plague, the Earl of Craven purchased land in a semi-rural area to the west of central London called Soho Field. He built thirty-six small houses 'for the reception of poor and miserable objects' suffering from the plague. Each night, death carts trundled through here and emptied dozens of wretched corpses into the earth. The area came to be known as Pesthouse Field following the burials but after that was referred to as Gelding Close, possibly from being the site of a stable, or from a tavern called the Gelding.

Due to fear and the possibility of lingering contamination, the land was left undeveloped for nearly ten years after the plague. It was given a new name too; it was felt that 'Golden' was more upmarket than the name 'Gelding', while the word 'Square' had a better ring to it than 'Close'. And so fashionable Golden Square was born. It was populated largely by aristocrats and Huguenot immigrants.

Golden Square was one of the last sites in the area to be developed, with the first building going up in 1705. In 1720, the historian Strype described the Square as a 'very handsome place railed round and gravelled with many very good houses inhabited by gentry on all sides'.

Those who have lived in No. 1 include Lord Maudaunt, who spent most of his time fighting wars in the Low Countries with the Duke of Marlborough's armies. The 4th Lord Byron, an ancestor of the poet who would be born a hundred or so years later, lived here also until the building and several adjoining ones were bequeathed to a foundation providing scholarships to children of the poor. The Bishop of Salisbury also resided here temporarily.

Between 1794 and 1861 a William Stodart, whose firm made harpsichords and pianos, took up residence here, beginning the site's musical heritage. Now Absolute Radio and Virgin Radio, which have been based at the same address since Virgin's launch in 1993, are resident in the building where children's ghostly voices are often heard in the basement, particularly after nightfall when the building is at its quietest. Sometimes shifting shadows in the dark of night cast gloomy shapes and there are those who say they have heard faint wailing which seems to come from beneath their very feet. But that should not come as a surprise to anyone; after all there is no escaping the fact that Golden Square is built on the site of a communal grave containing the bodies of around 4,000 wretched people.

New Scotland Yard, Parliament Street

The Prisoners Property Act of 1869 gave police the authority to retain certain items of prisoners' property for instructional purposes. This gave Inspector Neame the idea of starting a crime museum. He had already collected a number of items with the intention of giving police officers practical instruction on how to detect and prevent burglary. However, it was not until the Central Prisoners Property Store opened on 25 April 1874 that the opportunity presented itself to start a proper collection. The store was housed in No. 1 Great Scotland Yard at the rear of the Commissioner's Office at No. 4 Whitehall Place.

By then, Inspector Neame, with the help of a PC Randall, had gathered sufficient material from old and new cases to enable the opening of a proper museum. There was no official opening date in 1875 but the permanent appointment of Neame and Randall in the Prisoners Property Store on 12 April suggests that it came into being around then.

Two years elapsed before there was a record of the first visitors who arrived on 6 October 1877. They were Commissioner Sir Edmund Henderson KCB, accompanied by Assistant Commissioners, Lt. Col. Labolmondiere and Capt. Harris and other dignitaries. It was at this time that the name 'Black Museum' was coined after a miffed reporter from the *Observer* used the term when Inspector Neame refused to let him in for reasons unknown. The museum is now referred to as the Crime Museum.

The number of those who came to view the displays increased steadily and the first visitor's book (from 1877 to 1894) reads like a contemporary 'Who's Who'. Not every visitor was asked to sign the book but, as instruction in the museum was part of CID training, the museum was in constant use. Dignitaries to visit the museum included Gilbert and Sullivan, Sir Arthur Conan Doyle, Harry Houdini, The Prince of Wales (later to be Edward VII), Stan Laurel and Oliver Hardy, and Jerome K. Jerome.

In 1890 the museum moved with the Metropolitan Police Office to premises at the other end of Whitehall on the Victoria Embankment. The building, constructed by Norman Shaw and made of granite quarried by convicts on Dartmoor, was given the name 'New Scotland Yard'. The museum was housed in basement rooms here and, although there was no curator as such, PC Randall was responsible for adding to exhibits and vetting visit applications. In 1967, when the Metropolitan Police Headquarters moved to premises in Victoria Street, the museum was rehoused in rooms on the second floor, where it stayed until 1981 when a new, redesigned museum was opened on the first floor.

From Hell Letter, which reads: 'Mr Lusk, Sir, I send you half the Kidney I took from one women preserved it for you tother piece I fried and ate it was very nice. I may send you the bloody knife that took it out if you only wate a whil longer signed, Catch me when you can Mishter Lusk.' (wikimedia)

Given the nature of the collection which comprises some seriously grisly criminal exhibits, you might expect the odd visit from a spectre or two. When it was being renovated in 1874 a workman came upon the mutilated remains of a woman. A search of the area produced a foot and other body parts although weirdly, the head was never found. Later, in a dark and dusty corner, a crucifix engraved with the name of a convent was also discovered. From then on, officers and those who visited the building would report seeing fleeting glimpses in the basement of a shadowy figure – that of a headless woman dressed in nun's clothing, who always disappeared when approached. Some of those who sensed the spirit complained of 'something freezing cold' which pushed against their heads.

The museum, which closed during both world wars, covers two rooms containing a macabre collection of artefacts. One contains an extensive collection of weapons, all of which have been used in murders or serious assaults in London, and there are displays of items from famous cases, generally prior to 1900. A morbid display of death masks of people hanged at Newgate Prison sits on a high shelf and looks down impassively on visitors. On record is information about the first murder solved by using fingerprints, explosives used by nineteenth-century Fenian terrorists, and the IRA rocket launcher that was used to fire at the MI6 building in 2000.

The second room is brim-full of cabinets categorised 'Famous Murders', 'Notorious Poisoners', 'Murder of Police Officers', 'Royalty', 'Bank Robberies', 'Espionage', 'Sieges', 'Hostages' and 'Hijacking'. Cases detailed in the museum include that of serial killer Dennis Nilsen, and on display is his old white cooker, on top of which sits a battered aluminium cooking pot. No ordinary cooking pot, this, though: this is the same pot in which he boiled his victims' flesh before pouring it down his toilet. Nilsen is serving a life sentence for murder.

John Reginald Halliday Christie's dastardly deeds aren't forgotten either. Between 1942 and 1953 he murdered eight women – possibly more – in his house at 10 Rillington Place, Notting Hill. Christie collected women's pubic hairs and kept them in an old tobacco tin. He was found guilty of murder and hanged in Brixton Prison. The notoriety of the case led to Rillington Place being renamed 'Custom Close', though the buildings in the area were later demolished.

Part of the collection comprises shotguns disguised as brollies and walking stick swords – canes incorporating a concealed blade. The point of most of this gruesomeness on view is to show newly graduated police the dangers they face from disguised weapons.

Others mentioned in the displays include Ruth Ellis, the last woman to be hanged in Britain (13 July 1955) for murdering her lover. She had suffered a miscarriage just ten days before the killing after David Blakely had punched her in the stomach. The appeal judges ruled she had been properly convicted of murder according to the law as it stood at the time as the defence of diminished responsibility did not then exist. The 'Lambeth Poisoner', Dr Thomas Neill Cream's deadly exploits have not been forgotten either. Serial killer Cream was executed in 1892 after his attempts to frame others for his crimes brought him to the attention of police.

The museum, a sinister place, is not open to members of the public. It is a lecture theatre for subjects including Forensic Science, Pathology, Law and Investigative Techniques.

Some say that the entity which haunted the old premises still hangs around; that it moved with the museum exhibits. Certainly, something has been seen in the present museum, though descriptions vary. Some say they occasionally notice an otherworldly lingering smell of perfume, while a new recruit was terrified after he encountered the ghost of a former staff member.

Footnote: Although it is common knowledge that Scotland Yard is the HQ of the Metropolitan Police, few stop to wonder how it came by its name. Scottish kings visiting London in the sixteenth century stayed in an outpost of Whitehall Palace that came to be known as Great Scotland Yard. In the nineteenth century the name came to be linked with the Metropolitan Police as their first headquarters had a public entrance on Great Scotland Yard.

Admiralty House, SW1

Until 1964, the magnificent building of Admiralty House was the official residence of the First Lords of the Admiralty. Part of a complex of former Admiralty buildings, Winston Churchill lived here between 1911 and 1915, and again between 1939 and 1940. He was one of those visited by the persistent ghost of Martha Ray that has haunted generations of British politicians.

In the second half of the eighteenth century, Martha lived here. A good-looking, talented singer, she had a long-term affair with John Montagu, 4th Earl of Sandwich. She lived with him from the age of seventeen while his wife was suffering from mental illness and together they had five illegitimate children, one of whom was Basil Montagu, barrister, philanthropist and founder member of the RSPCA.

During this time, she had a successful singing career and completed her education with Lord Sandwich's support. He set her up in rooms at Admiralty House, providing her with a generous allowance. This gave her somewhere to stay during periods in which he did not wish her to remain at his home, although in public – though Sandwich was married – the two acted as husband and wife. During this period, Sandwich introduced Martha to a soldier, James Hackman. Within a short time he had become a frequent visitor to Martha's apartments and is thought to have proposed marriage frequently but she declined each time. By this time, Sandwich was deeply in debt and although he was financially generous to her, he did not offer her any long-term financial security, which may have been what led her to tolerate Hackman's advances.

Hackman left the army to join the church and became a priest, though by this time the pair were having an affair and James had fallen deeply in love with her. She, however, simply toyed with him; he was poor, of different social standing, and she wasn't interested in taking matters further. Hackman, by now completely infatuated with her, became ever more jealous and continued to pursue her.

On 7 April 1779, Martha went to the Royal Opera House in Covent Garden to see a performance of Isaac Bickerstaffe's opera, *Love in a Village*. A close friend, Caterina Galli, who was also a singer, accompanied her. Earlier that evening, Hackman had approached her, but she refused to tell him where she was going so he followed her. He believed that she had taken another lover, William Hanger, Baron Coleraine, whom Hackman witnessed her meeting at Covent Garden. (It is unclear whether she and Baron Coleraine were actually involved in an affair.)

Hackman was mad with rage and wildly jealous. He ran home to fetch a gun and returned to wait at the nearby Bedford coffee house until the show finished. At about a quarter past eleven, Martha Ray and Caterina Galli left the theatre. A large crowd was milling around in front of the theatre, and an Irish lawyer, John Macnamara, offered to escort them to their carriage. He led them through the crowd. Caterina Galli got into the carriage and Martha had one foot on the carriage step when James Hackman appeared.

According to Whig politician Horace Walpole it was at that moment that:

[James] came round behind, pulled her by the gown, and on her turning round, clapped the pistol to her forehead and shot her through the head. With another pistol he then attempted to shoot himself, but the ball grazing his brow, he tried to dash out his own brains with the pistol, and is more wounded by those blows than by the ball.

Martha died instantly. James then threw himself to the ground and began 'beating himself about the head' with the butt of his pistol whilst crying, 'For God's sake kill me!' James Boswell described the incident as 'one of the most remarkable that has ever occurred in the history of human nature'.

John Macnamara carried Martha Ray's body to the Shakespeare Tavern nearby, whilst James Hackman was arrested by a passing constable and taken into custody. His subsequent trial at the Old Bailey on 16 April 1779 drew a large crowd and a fee of one guinea was charged for admission to the public gallery.

James Hackman pleaded not guilty to murder, but pleaded temporary insanity and declared that he only intended to commit suicide.

Sandwich was devastated by her death, and Hackman was hanged for her murder on 19 April 1779 in front of a large crowd at Tyburn. Afterwards, his body was taken to Surgeons' Hall for public dissection in accordance with the Murder Act 1752. One man who viewed the dissection, Henry Angelo, later wrote that the experience had put him off pork chops for life.

Besides appearing several times to Winston Churchill in Admiralty House, Martha's ghost was considered 'part of the family' by politician Denis Healy in the late 1960s.

The Haunted Bed, the Victoria and Albert Museum, Cromwell Road

The Great Bed of Ware is on display in the Victoria and Albert Museum, and you can get up close and marvel at its immense girth and vast depths. The bed, which dates back to around 1590, really is massive, even by today's standards – measuring 10ft 9ins square and 7ft 6ins high. It is heavy, too, weighing 641kg (almost 101st). The Great Bed of Ware is probably the single best-known object in the museum's collections and is the only known example of a bed of this size.

The oak four-poster bed, carved with parquetry, was made by Jonas Fosbrooke, a carpenter from Ware and was originally housed in one of the local inns, though there are rumours that he made it for a member of the Royal Family.

Because of the town's position on the Old North Road, Ware became an important coach stop in the period between 1400 and 1700. It was a popular overnight destination for pilgrims on the route

Great Bed of Ware 1590–1760. (Victoria and Albert Museum)

from London to Walsingham, or travellers going to Cambridge University. In the *Canterbury Tales*, Geoffrey Chaucer mentions the town twice and named his notorious cook 'Roger Hogg of Ware'.

The bed's existence was first recorded in 1596 when a German prince stayed at the White Hart. Over the years, it came to be housed in several inns, the last being the Saracen's Head where it was kept until 1870. After that, the owner of the Rye House Hotel, Hoddesdon, bought it. The bed was acquired by the Victoria and Albert Museum in 1931.

The bed became so famous that is was mentioned by Byron in *Don Juan* and by Shakespeare in *Twelfth Night*, when Sir Toby Belch describes a sheet of paper as 'big enough for the Bed of Ware'. Reference was also made to it in Ben Jonson's play *The Silent Woman* (1609) and in George Farquhar's play *The Recruiting Officer* (1706) in which a bed is 'bigger by half than the Great Bed of Ware'. Visitors and those who slept in it often carved their initials on the bed or applied red wax seals, still visible on the bedposts and headboard today.

During its time in Ware, it was reputed to have accommodated '12 London butchers and their wives', probably as a dare, each of whom had to take care not to sleep next to an unrelated member of the opposite sex, otherwise he or she would itch for seven years. Some stories, probably exaggerated, say as many as twenty-six people have slept in it at any one time.

The bed was not only famous for its size but also for the fact it was haunted. Apparently anyone who tried to sleep in it was kept awake by 'the pinching, nipping and scratching that went on all night long'. The stories got so bad that people started to refuse to sleep in the bed. Who was the ghost involved? Many believe it was that of old Fosbrooke, furious that the hoi polloi were using his bed. Phantom fits of pique, in fact.

More Ghostly Snippets

- There is more chance of seeing a ghost between 1 and 3 a.m., as these are known as the 'hours of the dead'
- Children under the age of five are most likely to see a spectre
- There are times when ghosts attach themselves to objects rather than places and will follow these objects even if they are moved
- Not all ghosts are 'trapped' – some choose to stay within the earthly realm

4

EAST

'This melancholy London, I sometimes imagine that the souls of the lost are compelled to walk through its streets perpetually. One feels them passing like a whiff of air ...'

(W.B. Yeats, poet)

Wig and Pen Club, the Strand

It was London's only remaining drinking den for lawyers and journalists but then it gave up the ghost, so to speak, when

The Strand. (Library of Congress)

it closed in 2003. The 95-year-old Wig and Pen club, originally built in 1625 as the home of the Gatekeeper of Temple Bar, was the only structure in the Strand to survive the 1666 Great Fire of London. The Gatekeeper unwittingly began the catering tradition here by offering a 'pennorth of meat and bread' to the crowds who used to gather at Temple Gate.

The ghost of Oliver Cromwell, who was decapitated after death, is reputed to have visited the bar in the Club searching in vain for his missing head which was once displayed on a spike nearby.

Another apparition, that of a lawyer who committed suicide in the 1800s, has also been seen in the building.

Although the Club at number 230 has had a new lease of life and is now a Thai restaurant, a leaded stained-glass window bearing the date when it was built (1625) remains. It is inscribed with the most unlikely blessing ever to grace a haunt of lawyers and journalists: 'Go thy way, eat thy bread with joy and drink thy wine with a merry heart, for God approveth thy work.' There has been no sign of Oliver or the phantom lawyer since the Club changed purpose.

Coutts Bank, the Strand

Coutts Bank is London's largest private bank and boasts Queen Elizabeth II as its most illustrious client. It is probably true to say that a bank is probably one of the last places one would expect to find a ghost, but in November 1993 the directors took the extraordinary step of calling on the services of psychic medium Eddie Burks. They hoped that he would be able to lay to rest the phantom that was making a nuisance of itself in the computer room. Burks' amazing psychic powers made news headlines when he did just that.

A bank spokesperson told *The Times* newspaper that staff had reported 'strange happenings ... like lights going on and off'. There were also reports of an apparition described as 'a shadow' which appeared from time to time.

One unfortunate employee must have been scared witless when a ghost appeared before her minus a head!

A séance was held and the medium made contact with the restless, troubled spirit. He said it was Thomas Howard, 4th Duke of Norfolk (1538–1572), whose plot to marry Mary, Queen of Scots and depose Elizabeth I in Mary's favour resulted in his execution. 'I was beheaded on a summer's day,' the dejected Duke apparently informed Burks. 'I have held much bitterness and ... I must let this go. In the name of God I ask your help'.

Eddie Burks was able to persuade the spirit that the time had come for him to depart and on 15 November 1993, a congregation that included the present Duke and Duchess of Norfolk gathered at the nearby Catholic Corpus Christi Church in Covent Garden to say prayers for the repose of his soul.

Coutts Bank. (Mike Pickup)

Arundel House. (wikimedia)

On leaving the service, the present Duke was asked by a reporter if he was glad that his ancestor was finally at rest. 'Actually,' came the dismissive reply, 'I don't believe in ghosts.'

Footnote: But why would Thomas Howard haunt that part of the Strand? Lengthy research did not provide a definitive answer, though Arundel House, originally the townhouse of the Bishops of Bath and Wells, later in the possession of the Earls of Arundel, stood on the Strand until it was demolished in 1678. Arundel House came to the Duke of Norfolk from the Earl of Arundel by the marriage which united the Fitzalans and the Howards. Awash with art treasures known as the 'Arundelian Marbles' which included no less than thirty-seven statues and fragments of ancient art, this medieval pile with acres of grounds was the town residence of the Howards, Earls of Arundel and Dukes of Norfolk. Thomas, the 4th Duke of Norfolk, would have stayed here from time to time.

And Yet More Theatrical Ghosts

Before we go on to look at yet more spooky goings on in West End theatres, you might ask, why all the theatre hauntings? What is it about theatres that attract spectral activity? Theatres, like pubs, where lots of people gather over a number of years, often have a much higher than usual level of ectoplasm, built up over time, which enables spirits to materialise, be seen and sometimes heard.

That is, of course, only for those who believe in such things.

Adelphi Theatre, the Strand

Dating back to 1806, the Adelphi Theatre harbours a sinister story. A jealous bit-part player murdered actor William Terriss here in 1897, and a spectral William has returned to the theatre several times. Once, in 1928, he manifested himself to a tourist walking along the street, terrifying the man out of his wits. Nowadays, William's ghost is occasionally seen lurking in the wings though he also haunts Covent Garden tube station – more of which later.

William Terriss, who was born William Charles James Lewin, was something of an adventurer in his early days and travelled to the Falkland Islands, where he farmed sheep, the States, where he mined silver, and Bengal, where he cultivated tea. He returned to London in the 1880s when he decided to become an actor. He was immediately successful and soon reached a level of fame on a par with today's celebrity culture. Although flamboyant, the stage star was also noted for his generosity and willingness to help those less fortunate than he was. An example of this was when he turned up at the Adelphi one evening dripping wet. He wouldn't say why he was in this state, but later his fellow actors discovered that he had jumped into the Thames to rescue a child who had fallen in the river.

William also did everything he could to help a struggling young actor, Richard Archer Prince. He befriended him, lent him cash and helped him secure acting parts in his shows. Prince, however, was a heavy drinker, inclined to be violent and revelled in his nickname 'Mad Archer'. Despite William's support, Prince grew ever more envious and resentful of Terriss' success.

It reached a head one crisp winter's evening in December 1897. Terriss arrived at the rear stage door of the Adelphi by horse-drawn carriage. He leapt down and took a key from within his cloak to open the door to the theatre's private entrance, but before he could unlock the door, a figure leapt out from the shadows. Mad Archer threw himself at William, stabbing him ferociously several times.

Following the scuffle, a shocked crowd gathered and the famous performer was carried gently inside the theatre. Doctors were sent for from the former Charing Cross Hospital, now a police station on Agar Street, but within a short space of time William Terriss died in the arms of his mistress, actress Jessie Millward, in a theatre dressing room. As he died, he whispered, 'I will be back.'

Restrained by the growing mob, Mad Archer did not attempt to escape and calmly awaited his arrest, after which he was taken to a cell on Bow Street. The murder shook Victorian society. At the trial, Prince claimed that William had stopped him from advancing his career. The jury found him guilty, though he was spared the death penalty because they had decided that he was mentally ill. He spent the remainder of his life in Broadmoor Mental Institution, where he wrote and produced plays in which he always cast himself in the leading role.

Another bizarre event relating to the Terriss murder is that on the previous day, his understudy related a disturbing dream he had in which he had seen Terriss lying on the dressing room steps with blood flowing from a gaping wound in his chest.

Occasionally, the ghost of Terriss is seen pausing to knock on the door of what was once Jessie's dressing room.

A commemorative Blue Plaque on the stage door of the Adelphi reads: 'Hero of the Adelphi Melodramas who met his untimely end outside this Theatre 16 Dec 1897'.

More recently, comedian Jason Manford was surprised to encounter the spirit of William Terriss. Early in 2013, Manford was one of the guests on *Alexander Armstrong's Big Ask* on UK satellite channel Dave. During the show, Armstrong asked Manford, 'You had some weird experience in your dressing room, though, is this true?'

'I was in a haunted dressing room, yeah – well, I mean, if you believe in all that,' Manford replied and then went on to explain:

> I was talking to my daughter on Skype, she's three, and she was at home. And she just went, 'Daddy, what is that man doing behind you?' And I said, 'What? Wha – what does he look like?' And she said, 'He's a soldier.' I went, 'Hang on now, what's going on here?' But I spoke to the company manager at the theatre and apparently this guy was stabbed at the stage door in 1897, an actor, by an understudy but that night he was actually making his debut in a play called *Secret Service* when he was playing a lieutenant in the American Army. So, weird isn't it?

On the face of it, the wraith's appearance as a soldier fails to tally with previous sightings although *Secret Service* was indeed the play Terriss was due to star in. It later starred William Gillette, remembered for being the first man to play Sherlock Holmes, and it may be possible he took over the role when Terriss was murdered.

The phantom of Terriss has also been seen in a narrow alleyway leading to Bull Inn Court alongside the Adelphi. Actor Peter Wyngarde reported strange goings-on in his dressing room some years ago and these were put down to the ghost either of Terriss or of Ivor Novello, who some believe also haunts the Adelphi.

But why, you might ask, does William Terriss haunt Covent Garden tube station?

It could be because when William was alive, his favourite bakery stood here on the Long Acre site. He visited it on an almost daily basis. The station was not built until ten years after his murder.

The first sighting here of the phantom was reported on Christmas Eve 1955, when Jack Hayden, a ticket inspector, heard a knock on his office door. When he opened it, he found himself looking at the figure of a tall man, dressed in a grey frock cloak, homburg hat and white gloves, holding a cane. The man started at Hayden without saying a word, then just turned away and melted into thin air. Over the course of the next five or so years, Heyden spotted the same figure at least forty times, and ticket collector Victor Locker also saw the ghostly vision.

One night, a member of London Transport staff got the fright of his life when a white-gloved hand reached out of the darkness and touched him with icy fingers. However, it was only when a presence loomed up behind a station worker, terrifying him to the extent that he refused to come to work again, did London Transport decide to call in a spiritualist, Eric Davey, to come along and see what he could do. A séance was held and Davey contacted the spirit straight away. He said the name coming through to him sounded like 'Terry'. When he was shown a picture of William Terriss, the clairvoyant said he was in no doubt that was the man haunting the station.

Not that it got rid of the phantom though, as since then, London Transport employees have issued reports of a tall, distinguished-looking man walk climbing the spiral stairway, who dematerialises before reaching the top. On other occasions, the sound of voices is heard from behind a locked door and a man appears for a few moments before simply vanishing. The description is always the same – he is dressed in old-fashioned clothes, with a high-collared shirt and gloves. Occasionally, the sound of eerily echoing footsteps reverberate inside the station, though no one is visible. The ghost has also popped into the staff cafeteria, and although the last recorded sighting was in 1972, tube workers still sometimes report unexplained noises in the dead of night … but maybe, just maybe, some of the eerie noises have nothing to do with William Terriss' phantom – maybe there is another, or perhaps many other, peculiar goings-on in the bowels of this old station. Originally, this tube station was on part of the line opened by the Great Northern, Piccadilly and Brompton Railway. Right from the outset, there were stories of something strange about the Piccadilly line ploughing through this sacred square. At one stage, the local priest protested against the digging of the line because he believed that it would open up a gateway into hell.

Noël Coward Theatre, St Martin's Lane

Mind out for the ghost when you pay a visit to the Noël Coward Theatre. Formerly known as the Albery Theatre on St Martin's Lane, it opened in 1903 as the New Theatre. It was built by Sir Charles Wyndham and was later renamed the Albery Theatre in memory of the late Sir Bronson Albery, a previous manager. It underwent major refurbishment in 2006 and was renamed the Noël Coward Theatre when it reopened for the London premiere of *Avenue Q* on 1 June 2006. The spectral figure of Sir Charles Wyndham has been spotted lurking near the dressing rooms and occasionally he sits in the stalls to watch a show when there are not many people in the theatre. I wonder how he feels about all the name changes?

Duke of York's Theatre, St Martin's Lane

Violet Melnotte, known to everyone as 'Madame', was the first proprietor of the Duke of York's Theatre, the first of the three theatres to open in St Martin's Lane. In 1892, at the time when the theatre opened – it was called the Trafalgar Theatre then – St Martin's was literally a lane with muddy ditches on either side. Bad though it was, it had improved a great deal since medieval times, when the route was an open drain.

While alive, Violet enjoyed watching performances from her own box, and after her death in 1935 she has continued to do so. A presence, felt rather than seen, occasionally haunts her seating area. Actors have said she visits the green room too. Violet also sometimes appears in the dress circle bar, arriving as a wispy white mist developing into an outline. She usually announces her arrival there with loud knocking. Is she trying to communicate or just letting staff and actors know she is still there? No one knows.

But there was something a hundred times more unsettling than Violet's presence in this theatre. In the 1940s, it was the setting for the macabre 'Strangler Jacket' incident. The jacket, which was borrowed by the wardrobe department from the old Embassy Theatre, now part of the Central School of Speech and Drama, was a seriously frightening garment.

Actresses who wore the jacket during a production of *The Queen Came By* complained of feeling constricted and suffocated, as it seemed to grow tighter on the wearer; almost as if this black Victorian bolero was trying to squeeze them to death. During her fittings, the play's star, the late Thora Hird, had no problems with the jacket at the start, but once the show was underway, she said the garment seemed to grow tighter on her body.

However, the no-nonsense wife of the play's producer didn't believe in the allegations and wore the jacket herself to prove there was nothing wrong with it. When she took it off huffily saying, 'I knew it was rubbish, this is an ordinary jacket,' and handed it back to the dresser, she noticed the terrified look on the dresser's face. Turning to the mirror, she was horrified to see large red marks covering her neck, as if something invisible had tried to strangle her.

At a séance to try and get to the bottom of the matter, the sitters contacted the spirit of the actress who was first to wear it. She said that while she was wearing the jacket her boyfriend had strangled her, and then removed the jacket before putting the body in the river. It is almost as if the loathing the man felt towards her, as well as the method of killing, were absorbed into the fabric of the jacket, thus affecting those who have worn it since.

But where is the jacket now? British parapsychologist Peter Underwood discovered that it was sold to an American collector whose wife tried it on and immediately found it tried to strangle her too. Whether they kept the offending garment or not is not on record – one would think it is probably unlikely.

And finally, there is something else unworldly that happens in this theatre. Occasionally actors and staff have heard the sound of an iron fire door slamming shut, though the door in question is no longer there. An antique key once materialised out of thin air where the door used to be and fell at the feet of the then theatre manager. Scary stuff, but worse is to follow.

Lyceum Theatre, Wellington Street
Best beware when visiting the Lyceum Theatre. Prepare yourself for the possibility of seeing something that will surely freak you out. The phantom of an elderly woman sits in the stalls cradling a severed head in her lap. Who is she and whose head does she hold? Some accounts say that she is the spirit of Madame Marie Tussaud, who exhibited her waxwork creations for the first time in the theatre in 1802, and that the head is a wax model. This could well be the case.

One sighting during the 1880s, a couple watching a play happened to glance over the balcony and saw the severed head grinning up at them from the lap of a woman. Blood-curdling indeed, but they obviously lived to tell the tale because some years later the couple were visiting a house in Yorkshire when they spotted a portrait

Duke of York's Theatre. (wikimedia commons)

Lyceum Theatre. (wikimedia commons)

were "Is not this a lovely robe? It is so easy, and one does not have to wear corsets".'

Indeed, the dress itself is famous. Made from 1,000 iridescent wings of the jewel beetle – which the insects naturally shed as part of their life cycle – it has recently been restored at a cost of over £110,000 and is on display at the Costume Gallery in her home, the sixteenth-century house in Smallhythe Place, Kent, now owned by the National Trust. The cost of its restoration and re-display was met by donations, most coming from visitors to the house where she died in 1928.

And the last known Lyceum spectre is one we've encountered previously – William Terriss. In the Lyceum he is seen weeping, perhaps because he knows a return to the acting he loved is impossible. Terriss must be Covent Garden's busiest ghost.

of a man, with his head still attached to the rest of him. They recognised the face as that of the severed head they had seen years before in the theatre. The owner of the house explained the man in the painting was an ancestor, Henry Courtenay, Marquess of Exeter, who had once owned the land the Lyceum stands on and who was beheaded by Cromwell.

Actress Ellen Terry has also been known to put in the odd ghostly appearance here; perhaps not surprising as she played there for over twenty years up until her death. When this phantom appears she is wearing a sea-green Victorian dress, which she wore when she played Lady Macbeth in 1888. While she was in the role at the theatre, a male visitor to her dressing room said, 'There before me was Lady Macbeth in the glorious robe of green beetle wings ... Her face was wreathed in smiles, and almost the first words she said

Theatre Royal, Drury Lane

Joseph Grimaldi (1778–1837) performer and clown, still takes spectral curtain calls at the massive Theatre Royal in Catherine Street, Drury Lane. The character of the white-faced rogue with half-moons painted on his cheeks wearing an oversized harlequin suit became so popular that clowns are still referred to as 'Joeys' in his honour. Grimaldi's last request – gruesome in the extreme – was that his head be severed from his body before burial, which might account for his disembodied white-painted face having been seen several times watching a show over the shoulders of the occupants of one of the boxes. It scares the wits out of those who turn to find it eerily suspended in mid-air behind them.

There is a story about one of Grimaldi's appearances in 1807, when a deaf-mute man in the audience apparently found

Theatre Royal, Drury Lane. (Gilly Pickup)

the act so funny that his power of speech returned, and he shouted out, 'What a damned funny fellow!'

During his lifetime, the long-dead joker Grimaldi was an accomplished actor with an eye for the ladies, and who now enjoys more ghoulish fun by prodding unsuspecting actors, staff and cleaners. He is renowned for administering mischievous kicks, although he also likes to help aspiring actors too.

During the successful run of *Oklahoma*, an inexperienced American actress named Betty Jo Jones was alone on stage in front of a packed house but the laughter greeting her punchlines was disappointing. During one performance she felt hands on her shoulders which propelled her to a different part of the stage. The hands then gently repositioned her arms and adjusted the angle of her head. At the same time she delivered her lines to rapturous laughter. After the show she reported her experience but nobody in the cast, crew or audience had seen anyone but her on stage.

Oklahoma is obviously appealing to those in the spirit world because in 1948, during the show's run, a ghostly King Charles II and several of his courtiers suddenly appeared on stage for some seconds. Several actors and members of the public saw them.

The Theatre Royal was opened during the reign of this king who loved theatre, possibly because his favourite mistress, Eleanor (Nell) Gwyn, was associated with the theatre right from the time she sold oranges in the pit. Charles II also overturned a ban preventing women from performing on stage. Before the King's intervention, female roles including Juliet and Lady Macbeth were played by teenage boys. It is likely he did this to please his mistress, because soon after that she was promoted from orange seller to actor and made her first appearance as Cydaria in *The Indian Emperor*. From then on, she appeared on stage regularly, despite the fact that she could not read or write. Her last original character was Almahide in Dryden's *Conquest of Granada*. She spoke the prologue to this play in a straw hat, described as 'large as a cartwheel'. Charles II was present and was convulsed with laughter, though whether the mirth was due to the hat or Nell's acting we don't know.

Grimaldi's comforting hands were felt again years later by a novice singer auditioning on stage for *The King and I*. As she stepped onto the stage, the nervous girl felt a friendly pat on the shoulder and a phantom hand clasped her elbow before leading her to the front. All through her audition her hand was held by an eerie, disembodied force and despite the spooky guidance, the girl sang beautifully. She said she landed the role thanks to Grimaldi's calming influence. Actress Patsy Rowland, member of the cast in many *Carry On* films, said on occasion she heard phantom footsteps walk across the stage and was certain it was Grimaldi.

Grimaldi is not the only spectre treading the boards at what is the oldest working theatre in London and

Theatre Royal, Drury Lane. (wikimedia commons)

reputed to be the world's most haunted theatre. Although the present building dates from 1812, the first theatre on the site was founded in the 1660s, when Thomas Killigrew, one of Charles I's pages, obtained a licence to stage drama and took a lease on the land to build a playhouse. Sadly, it was burned down deliberately in 1672 by footmen who were cross that they were not allowed free entry.

Famed for supernatural shenanigans, the theatre is home to a veritable flock of phantoms including Dan Leno, former pantomime dame who went mad before his death in 1904. Actors and stagehands have been haunted by Leno's signature aroma of lavender – he used the scent to cover up his incontinence problem – before he gives them a push or pulls their wigs as they stand in the wings. If he is in a serious mood you may hear drumming coming from his dressing room where he used to rehearse his famous clog-dancing routine.

One of those who saw Leno's ghost was actor Stanley Lupino, who was insistent that he saw the phantom in his dress-ing room. It started with the feeling that someone else was in the room with him – and then he saw a dark shape walk across the room and straight through a closed door. The caretaker assured Lupino that there was no one else near his dressing room. However, shortly after that incident, when Lupino was again in his dressing room, he looked in his make-up mirror and was horrified to see, next to him, the white features of Dan Leno. Lupino was utterly petrified and immediately left the theatre. A few months later, Lupino was in the same dressing room with his wife when they saw Leno appear again. Apparently this was the last dressing room that Leno used in his lifetime. This story

was related by comedian Arthur Askey during a conversation he had with para-normal investigator Peter Underwood. Askey had no doubt at all that Lupino had the experiences he described.

However, the earliest spectre in this theatre dates back to 1735, when actor Charles Macklin murdered fellow actor Thomas Hallam over a petty argument about who should wear a certain wig. The argument turned nasty, and Macklin, who was known to be short-tempered, struck Hallam with his cane. It went through Hallam's left eye into his brain, killing him. As he took Hallam's life, Macklin shouted, 'God damn you for a blackguard scrub rascal!' Macklin was hugely popular and, although people witnessed the murder, he was sentenced not to death but to branding, though for some reason this was never carried out.

Macklin's ghost has returned from beyond the grave to be seen prowl-ing around backstage corridors. Those who have seen the presence describe seeing it as a 'corner of the eye moment' before the figure vanishes, but it is enough to make your heart rate scamper. Sometimes in the early evening, Macklin appears in front of what was the orches-tra pit, before the performance starts.

Another of the Theatre Royal's appa-ritions is the 'Man in Grey' who wears a powdered wig, tricorn hat, ruffled shirt, riding boots, a long grey riding cape and carries a sheathed sword. This handsome gentleman always sits in the end seat of the fourth row of the central gang-way in the Upper Circle for some time before getting up and walking straight through the solid wall. He never sits in a different seat and usually appears during mornings or afternoons while rehearsals are going on. He has been witnessed by countless people. In 1939, ghost hunter J. Wentworth Day reported seeing a moving blue light in the theatre, which he attributed to the Man in Grey. Unexplained draughts and the sound of running water often precede his appearances, but who was he in this life? It is believed that the ghost is that of actor Arnold Woodruff, who was murdered around 1790 and whose skeleton was found by builders during renovations in the 1870s when they broke down the wall he now walks through. They found a room containing a skeleton with a knife protruding from its ribs and shreds of grey cloth hanging from the bones. In 1939, the cast of Ivor Novello's *The Dancing Years* were gathered on stage for a photocall when the Man in Grey appeared before them, stalking his regular route. More than half the cast saw him. However, despite his bloody end, this ghost brings only luck as he only appears at the beginning of a successful run. These have included *The King and I*, *South Pacific* and every cast change of the long-running *Miss Saigon*. The late and well-loved Sir Harry Secombe, singer and comedian, along with his dresser, reported seeing the Man in Grey in the 1960s.

A number of otherworldly presences also share this theatre and Living TV's *Most Haunted* team filmed one of their blood-curdling episodes here.

Fortune Theatre, Russell Street
As if the Fortune Theatre's long-running stage play *The Woman in Black* is not hair-raising enough, the theatre is haunted by a woman, also fittingly dressed in black, who has been spotted in a lower box and in the hospitality bar. Actor Sebastian Harcombe claimed to have seen the figure of a shadowy woman to the right of the stage. He said it was obvious to him that this figure was that of someone from times gone by and not a living person. One leading lady mentioned that she felt she had been followed onto the

Theatreland. (VisitLondon images/Britain on View/Ingrid Rasmussen)

stage by someone she couldn't see, while other actors have whispered of shimmering apparitions which appear from time to time. Well, you know what they say – 'mortals live until they die, but ghosts hang around long afterwards'.

Vaudeville Theatre, the Strand

In the 2000s, a presence was often recorded in the Vaudeville Theatre. Over a period of about a year, box office staff said that from time to time the smell of a heavy herb-like perfume hung in the air, while backstage staff reported hearing noises and seeing presences. After the building had closed for the night, cleaners reported seeing a woman's feet and the bottom of a cloak floating just above the ground. The presence, who left a cold chill behind her, is thought to be that of a former actress.

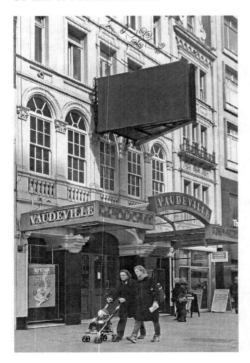

Vaudeville Theatre. (Gilly Pickup)

And here we go back briefly to William Terriss again. The foyer of this theatre had become infamous as the site of an argument in 1897 between him and Richard Archer Prince. Soon after that argument, the deranged Prince stabbed William Terriss to death at the stage door of the Adelphi Theatre. Prince, if you recall, was a struggling young actor whom Terriss had tried to help.

Peacock Theatre, Dean Street

Originally this was called the Royalty Theatre, and is where a woman dressed in an outfit dating from the Queen Anne period regally descends the staircase, slowly fading before she reaches the bottom. To chill your marrow further, when she reaches the bottom step, she unexpectedly gives a strident scream. But don't let it put you off paying a visit to the theatre, because the female spectre has not been seen recently. She seems to have been replaced by the sounds of a phantom dolphin which, during its life in the 1930s, was kept in a small tank under the stage – poor thing.

Coliseum Theatre, St Martin's Lane

In October 1918, there was a rather bizarre sighting – a group of people saw a man they recognised walking down an aisle in the Coliseum Theatre in St Martin's Lane. Although he looked like a real person, they couldn't believe it when they saw him simply disappear before them, leaving them in a state of alarm. Later, they discovered that he had been killed in trench warfare around the time they saw him. The soldier had spent his last evening on leave at the theatre. The entity, dressed in soldier's uniform, has been seen in the same area several times since on the anniversary of his death, 3 October.

Aldwych Tube Station

Finally, I'm including Aldwych tube station in this theatre section because it was built on the site of an old theatre – the Royal Strand, which stood here until 1905. Although no longer used as an underground station its well-preserved interior sees it often used as a film set. It has featured in many films including *The Battle of Britain* (1969), *Superman IV – the Quest for Peace* (1986), *The Krays* (1990), *Patriot Games* (1992), *Creep* (2004), *V for Vendetta* (2006) and *Mr Selfridge* (2013). The station façade was also used as a base-location in the BBC Three documentary series *Spy*, and it features on Level 12 of the Tomb Raider video game. Besides that, it is also a popular location for trendy parties and art exhibitions.

Its proximity to many West End theatres led to the running of special late night theatre train, gaining it the unofficial title of the Theatre Line. During the Second World War, its tunnels were used as air-raid shelters and to store various national treasures from the British Museum, including the *Elgin Marbles*. It was reopened after the war but finally closed on 30 September 1994, when the cost of refurbishing the lifts was deemed uneconomic.

The station, which has reverted to its former name of the 'Strand', is haunted by an actress who once trod the boards in the theatre which stood here. Over the years, numerous station workers claim to have seen her agitated presence late at night, wandering the station's deserted platforms and eerie, Stygian tunnels. Those who have seen and felt her appearances say they are preceded by an 'inexplicable atmosphere of oppression'. Others have reported the feeling of being followed by a 'nameless being'.

Strand Station. (Mike Pickup)

The Royal Opera House, Covent Garden

Often referred to simply as Covent Garden, this opera house and major performing arts venue is the home of the Royal Opera, Royal Ballet, and the Orchestra of the Royal Opera House. Originally called the Theatre Royal, it served primarily as a playhouse for its first 100 years. It incorporates parts of what was originally the Covent Garden Flower Market, which was absorbed by the main opera house in the 1990s.

It was during the £213 million reconstruction which took place between 1997 and 1999 that an unruly phantom started to cause trouble. For no apparent reason, scaffolding towers would rock uncontrollably and objects would fly through the air. Sometimes it seemed as if they were aimed directly at workers. The attacks usually occurred

The Royal Opera House. (VisitLondon images/Britain on View/Stephen McLaren)

during the day when up to 750 construction workers were on site. 'It's really spooky because no one ever sees the attacker, and the security is so tight no one could walk in off the streets. I was hit by a flying bolt last week – thankfully my hard hat took the impact,' said one senior employee.

Even after the work was completed, a bucket of bolts was picked up and hurled at a performer from the top of a lighting rig during a performance. At other times, spontaneously formed pools of water have appeared on the floor. Some say the poltergeist is Covent Garden personality Charles Macklin (who we met previously in this book as he also haunts the Theatre Royal, Drury Lane). Others prefer to think that it might be the spirit of a disturbed market worker, angry that the opera house has taken over the location of the old flower market.

But please don't be afraid if you pay a visit to the Royal Opera House; you are as safe as houses in this glorious building … or are you?

Non-Theatrical Ghosts

Seven Dials, Covent Garden

In the Middle Ages, the land that the Seven Dials stands on was a leper hospital. In the 1700s, this convergence of seven streets bustled with woodcarvers, straw-hat manufacturers, pork butchers, watch repairers, wigmakers and booksellers, as well as public houses. Though not as notorious as the dangerous St Giles 'rookery' – a 'rookery' was a slum – to the north, there were numerous incidents of mob violence in Seven Dials. By the middle of the eighteenth century, the area had declined to the extent that thirty-nine night watchmen were needed to be on duty every night to keep the peace, and by the early nineteenth century the area became infamous, together with St Giles, as one of the most notorious rookeries in London.

The centrepiece of Seven Dials is a column with six faces, each one a sundial, with the pillar itself forming a sundial that tells the time around the crossroads as the day goes by.

The spectral activity in this story dates back to the eighteenth and nineteenth century, when a rumour spread that the man behind the creation of Covent Garden, the Earl of Bedford, had been buried under the column with a haul of gold treasures. The rumour got so out of control that the authorities held a public exhumation of the non-existent 'grave' under the monument, showing that there was nothing buried underneath.

In those days, this was not the kind of area where riders or carriage drivers would stop for any unexpected obstacle – it was far too dangerous. As a result, fast-moving vehicles killed numerous late-night treasure hunters. Now on moonless nights there are those who say they have seen brief glimpses of figures who appear suddenly in the road, only to melt away as vehicle headlights fall on them. Are these the ghosts of those who journeyed to the poorly lit crossroads of Seven Dials in the hope that they would make their fortune from the buried treasure? Some like to think so.

The Lamb & Flag, Covent Garden

If you don't mind sharing your pint with a poltergeist, this is the place to come. A mischievous spirit occasionally causes a stir in one of London's oldest watering holes, the Lamb & Flag pub in Covent Garden, which dates to the 1600s. He – or it could be she – likes to move customers' belongings around the establishment. Charles Dickens often went in for a drink

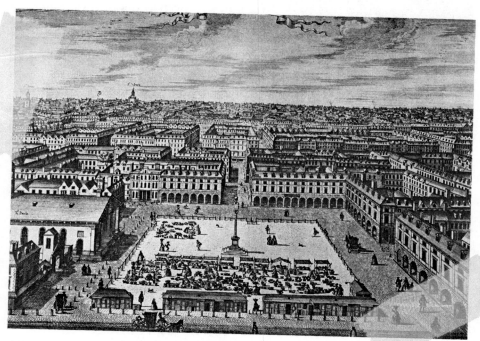

Covent Garden, around 1720. (wikimedia commons)

here in the 1800s, but which era the poltergeist comes from is unclear.

The venue has seen some of its less salubrious traditions slip through the net, including its reputation for fearsome bare-knuckle fighting, which earned it the nickname 'The Bucket of Blood'. Thankfully these days have gone. But on a wintry night in this pub, with its dark wooden bar and floor, high leather chairs, creaking joists, and the pale glow of moonlight glinting through a gap in the curtains, it doesn't take much imagination to believe there is a spirit or two lurking there.

Anne Lewis, who works as a marketing assistant in Covent Garden, said she was in the pub after work one evening with her friends Diana and Jodie. Diana went to the bar to place their order, taking with her only her wallet, leaving her handbag on a chair beside her friends. Jodie and Anne were chatting when Anne said she suddenly felt what she describes as 'a stifling feeling, almost like someone covering my face with a scarf or piece of material. I put up my hand to brush it away; I felt a sense of panic. It happened in an instant then it was gone. Jodie asked what the matter was as I'd stopped speaking mid-sentence. I tried to explain but she laughed it off.'

When Diana returned to her seat, however, no one was laughing. 'My bag – where is it?' she asked. She thought at first the others were playing a trick on her, but soon realised they knew nothing about it. At that, Jodie turned to see Diana's bag propped up behind the bar, beside the bottles of spirits. There was no explanation for how it got there, no one saw anyone move it. Anne doesn't believe in poltergeists, but says the incident was a 'scary mystery' with no obvious explanation.

Covent Garden

Covent Garden, originally called Convent Garden, is a 40-acre area once owned by Westminster Abbey. In the book *Ecclesiastical Antiquities of London*, the author tells us that 'the Abbot of Westminster had a garden on the banks of the Thames, where Westminster and London join, near St Clement Danes. It was called the Frère Pye Garden and stood opposite to the palaces of the Bishops of Durham and Carlisle.' The site is now Covent Garden.

Though mainly fields until the sixteenth century, the area was briefly settled when it became the heart of the Anglo-Saxon trading town of Lundenwic, the first major settlement to rise up in the wake of the Romans abandoning their fortress of Londinium in AD 46.

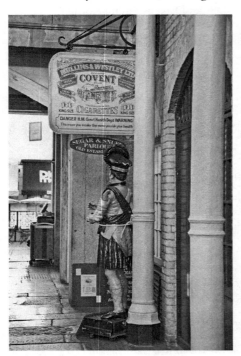

Historic shops in Covent Garden Market.
(VisitLondon images/Britain on View/Pawel Libera)

After the town was abandoned, part of the area was walled off by Westminster Abbey in around 1200, for use as a market garden and orchard. It was referred to as 'the garden of the Abbey and Convent'. The Abbot of Westminster managed it through the issuing of leases until the Dissolution of the Monasteries between 1536 and 1541, when it was taken by the state and eventually passed into the private ownership of the Earl of Bedford.

A nun from times gone by still haunts the area. Actor Bob Hoskins, star of films including *The Long Good Friday* (1980), *Mona Lisa* (1986), *Who Framed Roger Rabbit* (1988), *Mermaids* (1990), *Hook* (1991) and *Enemy at the Gates* (2001), had a strange experience whilst working as a porter in Covent Garden, during the period between 1957 and 1967. He explained:

I was down in the cellar at the time, when on the wall appeared a woman's face. She was wearing a nun's habit and reached out to me with upwardly turned hands. She spoke but I couldn't tell what she said. Later I learned that Covent Garden was once called 'Convent Garden' and was owned by the Benedictines of Westminster.

He said she was not a frightening figure, but was serene and looked kindly.

Other people walking in the area after dark have seen fleeting glimpses of a form dressed in a nun's habit. Indeed, sometimes people go to seek her out because it is said that those who see the phantom nun are blessed with good luck.

Former Gargoyle Club, 69 Dean Street

Number 69 Dean Street is a Grade II listed, eighteenth-century, four-storey Georgian town house, once home to the Gargoyle Club – a socially radical club and hangout of politicians, cosmopolitan intellectuals and artists. Founded in 1925, the Gargoyle dripped with decadence and lavish interiors, some designed by Henri Matisse. In its heyday, regulars included Fred Astaire and one of its members was the Duke of Windsor. However, by the 1950s it had degenerated into a seedy drinking den. Regulars included such well-known figures as Francis Bacon, John Minton and Lucian Freud.

In its day as the Gargoyle Club, it was haunted by one of King Charles II's mistresses, Nell Gwynn (or Gwynne), who once lived in rooms in a house on this site. The house built in 1632 was constructed above the Royal Saddlery near the Deanery in Soho, with the Royalty Theatre next door. Those who have seen her – and there have been many – describe her as a 'grey shadow, accompanied by an overpowering smell of flowers'.

Nell Gwyn by Simon Verelst. (The National Portrait Gallery History of the Kings and Queens of England)

There were also reports of a ghostly duel that took place on the roof of the building, between a Captain of the Guards and men sent by King Charles II to kill him. The duel scenario has not been witnessed now for around a hundred years. At the time of writing, the building is a hotel and restaurant.

Temple, WC2

This peaceful area of central London is one of the main legal districts of the capital and a centre for English law. Two of the four Inns of Court, Inner Temple and the Middle Temple, are here; the Royal Courts of Justice are to the north. The other two Inns of Court are Gray's Inn and Lincoln's Inn and every barrister in England has to belong to one of the four surviving Inns.

The Temple, a mixture of seventeenth-, eighteenth- and nineteenth-century buildings, is an almost hidden district of London, tucked away just off the Strand. The Temple area was originally the stronghold of the Knights Templar, those moneylenders, warriors and mystics who terrified Europe's crowned heads amid rumours of Satanism and black magic. Eventually, the Knights Templar were crushed, their orders broken up, members executed and their lands reallocated.

Quite when Judge Henry Hawkins started to haunt the Temple is not recorded, but this gentle ghost has appeared to some of those who visit the gardens. If you really want to see him, you must visit by yourself as he only appears when there is one person there.

Who was he in life? In 1898, Judge Hawkins was invested Baron Brampton. He liked to stroll leisurely around Temple gardens in his wig and gown; perhaps the peace helped clear his mind of everyday matters and legal problems. Often he was so deep in thought that he bumped into trees or people. After he died, this kindly person was remembered as a benefactor to the Church and society at large.

Although the Baron is no longer in this world, he still muses in Temple gardens. Never disturbing the calm, he simply strolls round. Some ghosts seem to have a habit of suddenly vanishing when seen, but not Baron Brampton, according to those who say they have seen this spectral figure – he glides at his leisure until he decides to move on by simply disappearing before their eyes.

Lower Robert Street

Sandwiched between the Strand and Victoria Embankment, Lower Robert Street is a narrow alleyway, rather sinister in appearance, sometimes nicknamed the 'Bat Cave'. Dating back to the late eighteenth century, the street was created as a by-product of 'The Adelphi', a development of twenty-four grand, terraced houses designed in the style of the ruined palace of Diocletian at Split in what is now Croatia. Scottish brothers John, Robert, James and William Adam developed the project and it got its name because 'Adelphoi' is the Greek word for 'brothers'. Construction began in 1772. The Scottish theme was in evidence with many Scottish labourers working on the project – hence why the sound of bagpipes was heard on an almost daily basis.

The 3-acre site had formerly been the grounds of Durham House, demolished after the Restoration when a network of courts was built. A series of arches and subterranean streets counteracted the slope from the Strand to the Thames. Lower Robert Street is now the only one of two remaining; the other is in the environment of the Royal Society of Arts on nearby Durham House Street.

The houses were luxuriously fitted with servants' quarters below, each of which had street access. Though there were problems with the foundations (they kept sinking into the mud) and a continual threat of flooding at high tide, it did not deter some wealthy and famous people from living in the Adelphi. Actor David Garrick, theatrical impresario and hotelier Richard D'Oyly Carte, social reformer Charles Booth, and literary figures George Bernard Shaw, Sir J.M Barrie and Thomas Hardy all had homes here. The Adelphi – and in particular the subterranean lair beneath – was also mentioned in Charles Dickens' *David Copperfield*: 'I was fond of wandering about the Adelphi, because it was a mysterious place, with those dark arches.'

In the late 1860s much of the Thames was reclaimed as part of an engineering programme to improve the city's sanitation. The Victoria Embankment was built in front of the Adelphi's lower vaults, depriving it of its prestigious riverside location. Once cut off from the Thames, the area rapidly fell into decline, with the arches being used to store coal and wine. In common with much of Victorian London, it became a haven for beggars and lowlifes with one historian noting: 'The most abandoned characters have often passed the night beneath the Adelphi, nestling upon foul straw.' Most of the Adelphi was demolished in 1936.

Lower Robert Street is just the kind of dark alleyway one might expect to be haunted. 'Poor Jenny' was a flower seller and prostitute who lived and worked here, her bed no more than a pile of rags. One night in 1875, a client strangled her. Now, occasionally a huddled, pathetic, rag-covered body materialises to scare the wits out of a hapless late night passer-by. Even more petrifying are the nightmarish screams that sometimes echo through Lower Robert Street, followed by the sounds of struggle before the air falls deadly silent. You will hear them if you time your visit right, and it will make your flesh creep.

19 Dunraven Street, Mayfair

There is more than a whiff or two of the spooky about this house in Dunraven Street. Originally it was No. 17 Norfolk Street and at that time its old

Lillie Langtry photographed by William Downey. (wikimedia)

walls reverberated to the spectral machinations of several ghosts including that of Jersey-born actress Lillie Langtry (1853–1929), lover of King Edward VII. Lillie, whose real name was Emilie Charlotte Le Breton, lived here between 1877 and 1880. London County Council renamed the street in 1939, because the 4th Earl of Dunraven and Mount Earl, a former resident of the street, was a member of the LCC.

In its time, the house and surrounding area has attracted several spirits, including Civil War cavaliers, a number of miscreants who were hanged at Tyburn and two phantoms who are headless. The reason for the numerous hauntings is unclear, though a nearby house was once the scene of a chilling murder where a butler cut his master's throat.

Lillie is a busy phantom, as she is also the resident ghost at Knightsbridge's Cadogan Hotel. Guests have seen her in the restaurant during quiet times and often at Christmas. From 1892, Lillie lived at No. 21 Pont Street, Chelsea, and when she sold the house it was absorbed into the Cadogan Hotel by the time it opened in the mid-1890s. Lillie remained there, living in her original bedroom, until 1897.

The Field of the Forty Footsteps, Bloomsbury

Before Torrington Square came into being, way back in the eighteenth century it was known as the Field of the Forty Footsteps. The area, part of meadowlands behind the British Museum, was originally called the

The British Museum. (VisitBritain/Britain on View)

Long Fields, then Southampton Fields. The story began when two brothers fell in love with the same woman, who would not declare a preference. Rather sadistically she watched as they fought over her 'so ferociously as to destroy each other; after which, their footsteps, imprinted on the ground in the vengeful struggle, were said to remain, with the indentations produced by their advancing and receding; nor would any grass or vegetation ever grow over these forty footsteps.' The blood they shed during their battle killed the grass and to this day it has never grown back. Sometimes in the dead of night, clashing swords are heard together with agonising cries of pain. Go if you dare.

In the early twentieth century, writer and spiritualist Jessie Adelaide Middleton investigated the legend and believed that she had established the precise location of the mysterious footsteps. She wrote:

I often wonder if those who sleep calmly and peacefully in the quiet lodging-houses of Torrington Square ever guess that the ground over which they are sleeping was once the scene of a desperate tragedy... As regards the exact locality, I have taken great pains to confirm it, and from various sources have ascertained that no doubt it covered what is now Torrington Square ...

Still more Ghostly Snippets

- There are different kinds of ghost – poltergeists, spirits, full or partial apparitions, demons and orbs
- More ghosts are sighted in pubs than anywhere else
- Animals and children are more likely to 'see' a ghost
- Spirits can often be protective of the families they haunt

5

WEST

'From ghoulies and ghosties and long-leggety beasties / And things that go bump in the night, Good Lord, deliver us!'
(Anonymous)

Handel House Museum, 25 Brook Street

In the summer of 1723, George Frederic Handel moved into the newly built house at what is now No. 25 Brook Street in Mayfair. He lived there for thirty-six years and died in the upstairs bedroom in 1759. Fast forward to the year 2000, when the upper storeys of the building were leased to the Handel House Trust.

On 8 November 2001, the Trust made an announcement: 'Handel's spirit was brought back ... when the Handel House Museum opened to the public.' Perhaps a somewhat unfortunate turn of phrase, because during the restoration project there were indeed reports of a spirit – of an ethereal kind – haunting the building. In 2001, the hauntings were considered bad enough for the Handel House Trust to call upon the services of a local priest to see if he could lay to rest the ghost that had been seen by at least two people.

Handel House by Andreas Praefcke.
(wikimedia commons)

'We weren't sure whether having a ghost would attract or deter customers,' commented Martin Egglestone, a trust fundraiser, who twice encountered the apparition in the room where Handel died. In June 2001 he was helping measure up for some curtains when he reported that 'suddenly the air got very thick'. The next moment, a shape that resembled 'the imprint on the back of your retina when you close your eyes, having been looking at the sun for too long' appeared before him. Mr Egglestone described the apparition as female and quite tall. He observed that 'there was no malevolent feeling. It felt like the pressure you get when you brush past someone in the Tube and they are too close to you.' The sighting was confirmed by another employee. Staff also reported a strong, lingering scent of perfume hanging in the air of that bedroom.

Although Handel lived alone, sharing his home only with his manservant, two sopranos frequently visited the house – Faustina Bordoni and Francesca Cuzzoni, divas both, who vied with each other to perform in his operas. 'There is a possibility that the ghost might be one of them,' said Mr Egglestone, 'but they would probably have sung in the room in which he had his harpsichord on the floor below the bedroom.'

Interestingly, the upper storeys of No. 23, next door, which are now part of the Handel House and the museum and used for changing exhibitions, was the home of rock legend Jimi Hendrix from 1968–9. He also claimed to have seen a ghost on the premises while he lived there.

A local priest, who wished to remain anonymous, said water was sprinkled and a prayer read out to try to send the apparition away. 'This is a soul who is restless and not at home,' he told the *Daily Telegraph*. 'I don't see it as evil or horrible and one should help it to be at peace.'

The Masons Arms, Upper Berkeley Street

An icy chill sometimes hangs in the air of this pub. Centuries ago, prisoners on their way to meet a terrible death at Tyburn gallows at Marble Arch were thrown into a small prison cell in the basement of what is now the Masons Arms prior to being taken to execution. These days a blocked-off tunnel still connects the basement of the pub to old dungeons at Marble Arch. Legend has it that the ghosts of these tortured beings still make their presence felt at night in the basement of the pub when the witching hour approaches. One should not expect less, given the building's sad history.

Masons Arms. (London on View/VisitBritain)

Volunteer Pub, Baker Street

Reeking of a bygone era, the Volunteer pub, which got its name because it operated as a recruiting station during the war, was built on the site of a grand seventeenth-century mansion. The mansion was one of the homes of the aristocratic Neville family until the mid-1600s when the building burned down. Several of those who were in the house perished in the fire. The cellars were all that remained, and these form the foundations of the pub today, and it is here that the ghost walks.

Research tells that the spirit is that of Richard Neville. He is dressed in surcoat, breeches and fancy stockings, and this particular haunting is mentioned in *The Haunted Pub Guide* by Guy Lyon Playfair (1985): 'it was seen on a number of occasions in the 1960s by landlord Joseph Gardiner as well as by some of his customers, and according to a paranormal researcher it is thought to be that of a former resident, not of the building itself, but of the site.'

Gardiner himself did some research on his ethereal guest, his interest aroused by a clear sighting of a figure he saw in the cellar not long after some rebuilding work had been completed. Lights would flash off and on inexplicably and even the power failed for no reason. Gardiner figured that the clothes his ghost was wearing were appropriate for that period. Sky TV's *Most Haunted* team visited to try to contact this posh spirit but he didn't play ball during their time in the pub.

The Grenadier, Mayfair

The prize for London's most haunted pub, if there were such a thing, would

The Grenadier. (Mike Pickup)

surely go to the Grenadier. This public house, tucked away in a quiet mews, has in fact been named the world's most haunted pub, but perhaps for those who are sceptical about such things, a visit or two at the appropriate time might just change their minds.

A tragic spirit, that of a young soldier who was stripped and flogged to death here after he was found cheating at cards, haunts this pub in one of London's most affluent quarters. On one wall, yellowed newspapers tell of the Grenadier's haunted history, and a small crucifix hangs on a wall of the cellar to ward off harmful spirits or energies.

The upper floors were once the officers' mess of a nearby barracks, while the cellar was a gambling lair for the soldiers. Although the year in which the murder occurred is not known, it almost certainly happened in the month of September, as this is when the pub experiences an onslaught of supernatural activity. Clouds of cigar smoke appear from nowhere and various levels of poltergeist-like activity occur, including the disappearance of objects, the unexplained movement of tables and chairs, and drawers moving in and out of furniture of their own accord. Footsteps resound in empty rooms and occasionally a ghostly sound of someone sighing comes from the cellar. Several years ago, when a Chief Superintendent from New Scotland Yard was enjoying a drink in the pub, wisps of smoke began to waft around him. His curiosity aroused, he reached towards the apparent source of the smoke and with a cry of pain, pulled his hand quickly back as an invisible cigarette burnt it.

Customers have described the spirit as 'an indefinable but definite atmosphere' and it has affected both people and animals. The son of one landlord said he saw a 'black shape' outside his bedroom one September evening, while a landlady says she saw a figure coming up the stairs which suddenly vanished. Several years ago, a visitor, staying there for a few nights, saw someone standing beside his bed before they disappeared.

One former relief manager, Peter Martin, said at around midnight one night, when he was in the bar with a colleague, they both saw a bottle lift itself from approximately 1ft from the floor where the box of mixers were kept to head height, where it exploded. He also spoke of keys which had a habit of disappearing, only to reappear in a different place.

A head barman at the pub in the early 1980s told a tale about the ghost:

One busy winter's night about 8.30 p.m., I went down to the cellar to fetch some cigars. At the foot of the cellar steps to the left was a wooden 'lock up' about the size of a garden shed that served as the spirit and tobacco store. Built into a corner of the cellar, this structure comprised two wooden walls and two brick walls. On busy nights it was almost impossible to get a cigarette break, so I would sometimes keep a cigarette in a glass ashtray in the lock up and sneak a couple of drags when possible, as I did on this occasion.

As if from nowhere, Bobby, the landlord's friendly black cat appeared. This was unusual as he wasn't allowed out of their flat during opening hours, let alone allowed to roam the cellars. As I stood there, several things happened. The temperature plummeted, Bobby arched his back and sunk teeth and claws into my leg and the ashtray, which was on a chest high shelf to my left, flew past my head and smashed with significant force against the wall beside the bricked-up tunnel. I felt a bone-deep chill of fear that I have seldom experienced since and needless to say exited the cellar at the velocity of a Polaris Missile. At the top of the cellar steps, back in the warm ambience upstairs, I felt silly – maybe I imagined it. As I stepped behind the bar someone said, 'Are you alright, you look like you've seen a ghost?'

In September 1991 a break-in was reported at the Grenadier. A number of items had been thrown across the lounge area, and drawers had been emptied and the contents strewn over

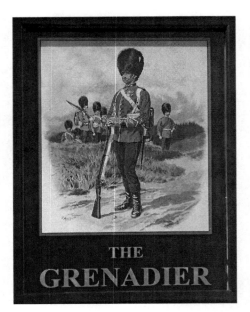

The Grenadier. (Mike Pickup)

the room, but nothing had been stolen. The strange thing was, several people had been sleeping in the building that night, but no one heard anything.

In the early 1990s, BBC's *Six O'clock* show ran a programme on London's most haunted pubs and the Grenadier was featured. A couple of weeks later, a photographer brought in some 'stills' of the event. There was a fuzzy image in one of the window panes that vaguely resembled a face. The photographer was cynical and had the photograph blown up and zoomed, which made the face clearer than before, though still vague. Once more, the photographer had zoomed in and there was the face of a man with a handlebar moustache, wearing what appeared to be a fez-like hat. The face appeared to be looking straight at the photographer.

The Grenadier is consistently listed among the top ten most haunted pubs in Britain and has attracted some well-known names, including, it is said, Madonna and Prince William, though probably not due to the spectral activity.

Hyde Park Corner Tube Station

Hyde Park Corner tube station is one of the few London Underground stations with no associated buildings above ground, so it truly is an 'underground' station. It has a hair-raising story connected to it too.

In November 1978, Barry Oakley, the Station Supervisor, was working the night shift at Hyde Park Corner. It was late and the station had been closed to the public for several hours. Having checked that he had properly removed the breakers – a piece of equipment designed to stop escalators from moving – he and a colleague returned to their office.

All was normal until about 2.30 a.m., when they heard what they later described as 'a commotion' in the booking hall area. The men went to investigate and could not believe their eyes when they saw an escalator moving. This was extremely odd because there was no power going to the escalator and a special key is required to start it running. An hour or so later they both returned to the office. They had conducted a thorough search to try to find out what had caused the noise, but could shed no light on it.

Feeling more than a little spooked at the strange events, Barry went to put the kettle on. As he did so, he had the strangest, most intense feeling that the eyes of an invisible presence were boring into him. At the same time, the temperature grew icy, so much so that he said afterwards he could see clouds of his breath as he exhaled.

Sharply, he turned round to see that his colleague had turned deathly pale and was clearly very distressed. Shaking from head to foot, he said a disembodied head had floated through the office wall and had stopped to watch them both. At that, he rose, said to Barry that he was leaving and would never return to work at that station again. He remained true to his word.

But what about the ghostly head? It seems to have disappeared without trace, or at least no more strange incidents have been recorded at that station.

228 Baker Street

Sarah Siddons was a commanding performer. In fact, the eighteenth-century actress' performances were so authoritative that audiences swooned. Occasionally people even had to be helped out of the theatre in various stages of distress. In the words of essayist William Hazlitt, Sarah Siddons 'was tragedy personified'.

Sarah lived in a house at No. 27 Upper Baker Street until she died in 1831. Though the house was demolished in 1904 to make way for the underground station, her apparition was seen several times during the rebuilding at what is now No. 228 Baker Street. The inspection gallery on the top floor would have been the approximate location for Sarah's former bedroom and this is where many of those working there saw her. Most of the reported spectral activity took place during the day.

While the house was being demolished, an article about 27 Upper Baker Street, called The 'Tragic Muse' appeared in the *Otago Witness* (a New Zealand newspaper that ran between 1851 and 1932):

Railway extension has caused the disappearance of many old landmarks, and it now claims the ground on which stands No. 27, Upper Baker Street, a house round which cluster many memories of the London stage. It was here that Mrs Siddons retired to rural peace and quietude from her triumphs on the boards. She bought the house, then almost the last in London, and built a big bow window from which she could look over the green fields and hawthorn-bowered lanes which stretched away towards Finchley. And here the last years of her life were spent, pleasantly enough. She had realised a handsome fortune. The memoirs of the time are full of references to the 'Tragic Muse' as she loved to be styled. Washington Irving tells how he would walk to Baker street to hear her read passages from Shakespeare in that voice of 'thunderous music' by which she had been used to hold the crowded houses spellbound.

It seems Sarah likes to get around in ethereal form: she is also reputed to haunt the Bristol Old Vic and the Sarah Siddons School on North Wharf Road, London.

Vine Street, W1

At one time, Vine Street's main claim to fame was its police station, which came into existence in 1829 with the creation of the Metropolitan Police. Said to have been the busiest in the world, this was where the Marquess of Queensberry was charged with criminal libel against Oscar Wilde in March 1895, the basis for the series of events that eventually led to Wilde's imprisonment.

Vine Street police station remained operational until the West End Central police station on Savile Row was opened in 1940. That same year, the former Vine Street police station reopened as the Aliens' Registration Office. Shortly after this, the street name was changed to Piccadilly Place. However, owing to a shortage of space at West End Central, the old police station reopened in 1971 and Westminster Council agreed to resurrect the street's original identity, so that the station could retain the Vine Street name. The police station has now been replaced by a mixed-use development.

The building was – or perhaps still is – haunted by a police officer who lived in Streatham, Sergeant Goddard. He was charged on a warrant granted under the Corrupt Practices Act and knew he would lose his job. He hanged himself in a cell in 1928.

After his death, those working in the police station regularly heard what sounded like heavy boots patrolling the corridors, and saw cell doors mysteriously open and clang closed again. One officer, who walked along the corridor to try to find out the cause, realised that what he thought were his footsteps echoing on the stone floor was actually a separate set of footsteps following him, though no one was visible. One time, spectral activity took place almost nightly, while a figure dressed in old-fashioned police uniform could be seen looking into the cell in which Goddard died.

Green Park

There is a legend that Sir Henry Colt and fellow duellist Beau Fielding still meet here from time to time to fight for the love of the Duchess of Cleveland. The story goes that should you happen to be in Green Park early on a misty morning, you might just hear the sounds of heavy breathing and the clashing of swords … but this story is not about aristocrats fighting a duel, it is about a particularly scary tree.

Granted, it isn't often that you happen upon a haunted tree, but there was one which grew in Green Park. While Dutch elm disease eventually finished it off, rumours of eerie presences where it once stood continue. This may not be as odd as it seems, as there were those who hanged themselves from this 'tree of death'.

Sometime in the 1930s, a tramp called Black Sally met a dreadful end as she slept underneath the tree canopy. She was brutally stabbed by something or someone unknown. The story goes that Sally had ignored warnings not to sleep beneath this tree where mysterious things had a nasty habit of happening – whispers abounded that people who had fallen asleep beneath it never woke up again. Birds shunned this tree. There was no cacophony of birdsong here; they never lingered on its branches and unlike most of the other trees in the area, no wild flowers would grow beneath it. Maybe there is another strange explanation for the lack of flowers which grow in Green Park though, because the park covers the burial ground of a leper hospital.

In the early 1900s, Elliot O'Donnell, a prolific Irish author who wrote books about ghosts and who died in 1965, got into conversation with a tramp in the park. The vagrant, clothes worn and thick with grime, described spending a night underneath this haunted tree with branches that seemed to shiver like a spider's web. He said he was woken by

A creepy tree. (Gilly Pickup)

deathly cries of 'Oh God!' and sounds of awful, unearthly groaning. Thinking someone had been attacked nearby he stood up but, despite the halo of a bright moon, could see no one. Fearing something supernatural, he fled and slept at the other side of the park on a bench. O'Donnell recorded the encounter in his classic book, *Trees of Ghostly Dread*. Later, he was told by other tramps that they always shunned the cursed tree. If only Black Sally had heeded the warnings and done the same.

On another evening, Elliott was walking through the park when he heard the distant sound of a fiddle. He followed it, wondering who was playing so late, until he came to a clump of trees where he met a policeman. The policeman told O'Donnell that he 'would never find the fiddler' and recounted the following tale which he had been told:

An old fiddler found a tree to sleep under in the park and when he awoke he realised his fiddle had gone. It was all he had in life so spent his time wandering round the park asking those he met if they knew where his fiddle was. In fact, he was later reunited with his beloved instrument – but only after he was dead. He hanged himself with his braces from a tree and from then on the clump of trees where the fiddler died had ghostly fiddle music emanating from it.

And an important footnote to this story: Be careful if you go to Green Park and pause to rest on a park bench. It isn't just a ghostly tree you should watch out for. You might just find yourself sitting next to the phantom of a wild-eyed man desperately trying to cut his own throat with a razor.

The Georgian House Hotel, St Georges Drive

One day in 1989, the manager of the Georgian House Hotel was showing a visitor round when they heard the sounds of children laughing and scampering along the corridors, chattering, shouting and banging the fire doors. Irritated, the manager went to ask the receptionist to tell the children's parents to keep the noise down. But – and here's the strange thing – no guests had checked in that day and there were no children in the hotel!

William Chinnery Mitchell built the Georgian House Hotel as a private house in 1851, and the current family owners are his direct descendants. The hotel comprises three houses in St George's Drive and one smaller house in adjoining Cambridge Street, named the Bower House.

At times, this hotel has been awash with ghostly happenings. Paranormal occurrences have been witnessed and sudden icy blasts of air have been felt when there were no windows open, voices have been heard coming from empty rooms, as well as footsteps fading down corridors or climbing stairs.

In 1991, a new member of staff was allocated one of the guest rooms to stay in before moving into staff accommodation. The next morning she was extremely annoyed with the manager. 'Why has a copy of my room key been given to someone else?' she asked angrily. When asked to explain, she said that she woke up in the night to see an old man sitting at the foot of her bed. When she enquired what he was doing there, he did not reply, but simply stood up and walked out of the room. The nonplussed manager told her that no one else had a copy of the key and no old man such as she described was staying at the hotel.

In 1998, some repairs were being carried out in the hotel when two workmen reported sudden freezing cold blasts of air and said that they felt a strange presence in the room, unusual for tough builders working in summer!

In 2007 a staff member said that she heard people laughing and talking in the dining room, but when she went in, there was no one there. Since then, this has happened several times.

One night in 2008 the porter heard footsteps going upstairs and walking along the corridors. He went to check who it was but – lo and behold! – there was no one there. Besides these incidents, there have been various reports from staff and guests who have seen, heard or felt something unusual in the hotel.

Several members of staff have seen a male spectre in one of the basement staff rooms. Is this is the same ghostly figure that has appeared in the kitchen and one of the top-floor bedrooms? No one is sure.

To go back for a moment to the ghosts of the children mentioned at the beginning of the story. Since 1989, they have occasionally appeared on the upper floors of the building. One manageress even held a conversation with them and assured them that, since the hotel is a friendly and hospitable place, they were more than welcome to visit, but she asked only that they confine themselves to the upper floors since their presence on the lower levels might prove disturbing to their real-life peers.

It seems certain that there are ghosts in that building, but over the years these presences have been benign ones, adding to the welcoming atmosphere of the hotel. If you want more than a fair chance of seeing something otherworldly, then Rooms 10 and 12 are rumoured to be the most haunted.

Montpelier Street/Square, Knightsbridge

In 2009, American actress and singer Miley Cyrus, together with members of her family, upped sticks and moved to a hotel after experiencing creepy shenanigans in an apartment they were renting during the singer's European tour. The apartment, which is quite close to Harrods, stands on the site of an old bakery, and the singer and her family witnessed some strange happenings during their brief stay there.

The *Daily Mail* reported that she said, 'it was seriously so terrifying. The apartment used to be an old bakery before it was turned into an apartment building, and I was having really weird dreams about scary things.' She went on to say that one night, when her younger sister was in the shower, she heard her scream. Miley ran into the bathroom to find the tap had switched over by itself to 'hot' and the water was burning her sister.

The singer says that another day she experienced a ghostly sighting. 'I thought I saw a little boy sitting on the sink, kicking his feet, watching me take a shower and I felt really freaked out.'

She said that bizarre things kept happening in the house and her fiancé, Liam Hemsworth, experienced strange happenings, as did her aunt. The latter said, 'I have no idea what happened but I left the apartment and when I came back all the doors and windows were open. I know that I locked everything before going out.'

Harrods, near to the flat which popstar Miley Cyrus said was haunted. (Britain on View)

Miley said, 'We found out that a man who owned the bakery lived there with his son and then the dad died and the son took over the bakery. I think I was seeing the son.' Deciding enough was enough, the singer and her family packed their bags and moved to the Soho hotel. Historical accounts of the area say:

1838 when the plots formed part of a demise to Charles Bowler, a Fetter Lane baker, still unfinished No. 43 was leased to a grocer in March 1839. A grocer and cheesemonger's shop throughout the 1840s, it was taken over about 1850 by a young Scottish draper, and a drapers it remained. This shop and the pub, with the dairy and the stationers over the road and later a general practitioner at No. 42, gave to this corner a business character of which no trace remains.

The Embassy of Finland, Belgravia

The Embassy of Finland at No. 38 Chesham Place dates from the 1830s. At that time it was a private house, not an Embassy. In the beginning, the building was called Herbert House and after that, it became Belgrave House, and the following haunting has its roots in the days when it was a private residence.

The first recorded resident of No. 38 Chesham Place was a Major General James Ahmuty. By 1881, Mary Elizabeth Ashe à Court-Repington Herbert, Baroness Herbert of Lea — since the name is rather a mouthful she was known simply as Lady Elizabeth Herbert — was living here, and this is where she died thirty years later.

Subsequent occupants include William Russell, a relation of the 1st Earl Russell, who served twice as prime minister and who lived close by at No. 37 Chesham Place. During the Second World War, the British Red Cross Society and St John's War Organisation occupied the house, and between 1947 and 1948 the Victoria League for Commonwealth Friendship took over the lease. When they surrendered their lease in 1975, Belgrave House became the Embassy of Finland.

There is no record of whether any of the previous occupants happened upon a ghostly figure, but certainly since 1975 some staff members in the Finnish Embassy have reported paranormal sightings which are always preceded by a thickening silence and a dramatic drop in temperature. It is said that the ghost is that of a little girl who accidentally fell from a third-floor window of the house in the 1800s. The room she fell from was a nursery.

One staff member, who worked in the Embassy with her husband, said, 'My husband, a serious sceptic, had to change his mind about ghosts when he witnessed various incidences of paranormal activity. Others have also seen the ghost of the child on the stairs in her nightdress.'

Apsley House, Hyde Park Corner

Apsley House is one of the grandest Georgian buildings in the metropolis. Known as 'Number One London' (it was the first building encountered on the road to the city after the toll gates at Knightsbridge), it was the London home of the Duke of Wellington after his victory over Napoleon at Waterloo.

The house has one of the finest art collections in London, with paintings by Velazquez and Rubens and a stunning collection of silver and porcelain, though pride of place surely goes to a massive nude statue of Napoleon. Today, it is open to the public as a museum and art gallery, although the present Duke of Wellington still uses the building as a part-time residence. This was where the ghost of Oliver Cromwell made a dramatic appearance to the Iron Duke one chill winter's night in the 1830s.

At the time of Cromwell's eerie appearance, angry crowds were rioting outside Apsley House. The furious mob was there because of the Reform Bill which was opposed by the Tories and the Duke, who was then prime minister. The people were angry because at that time, only the rich and wealthy middle classes had the vote and they felt enough was enough — the Tories had been in power for almost sixty years, but at the

Apsley House. (wikimedia commons)

latest election had merely scraped in. Still, the Duke of Wellington declared in the House of Lords that he was opposed to any reform of parliament.

As Antonia Fraser wrote in her book, *Perilous Question: The Drama of the Great Reform Bill 1832* (Weidenfeld), the Duke 'suffered from the isolation which haunts the very grand'. She goes on to say he badly misjudged the public mood, which strongly supported reform; his government fell, the mob took to the streets, and Wellington ordered armed men to defend the windows of Apsley House.

Not quite knowing which way he should turn and in the knowledge that the crowds were baying for his blood, the Duke suddenly found himself looking at an armour-clad figure. He recognised the man from portraits as Oliver Cromwell. Cromwell said nothing, but pointed dispassionately to the crowds outside as if to tell the Iron Duke how foolish he was being.

The Reform Act was passed by a small majority on 13 April 1832. The Whigs – who had been out of power for so long that they seemed condemned to permanent opposition – took office, and Lord Grey formed a minority government, pledged to the reform of parliament. Wellington's fall had provided him with the chance he was waiting for and the people got their wish for reform.

It was not until years later, however, that the Duke told anyone about his spectral encounter. As far as we know, Cromwell did not make further appearances in the house.

Theatre Royal, Haymarket

It seems that actor-managers like to keep an eye on things in their theatres even after they are no longer alive. Acclaimed performer John Baldwin Buckstone who lived in the mid-nineteenth century, still

Theatre Royal, Haymarket. (VisitLondon images/Britain on view)

Theatre Royal, Haymarket. (Gilly Pickup)

likes to come back from time to time to visit Number One dressing room at the Theatre Royal Haymarket. A friend of Charles Dickens, Buckstone wrote and performed mainly comedies and farces. Although he has not been in this world for many years, members of staff have heard a man's voice rehearsing lines in his former dressing room. On opening the door of course, the room is empty.

Waiting for Godot opened here on 30 April 2009, with Sir Patrick Stewart and Sir Ian McKellen playing the lead roles. Their performances garnered critical acclaim, and were the subject of an eight-part documentary series called *Theatreland*, produced by Sky Arts.

The *Daily Telegraph* reported that Patrick Stewart saw Buckstone's ghost.

Coming offstage for the interval, Sir Ian asked him, 'What happened, what threw you?'

'I just saw a ghost. On stage, during Act One,' Stewart replied. He told his co-star that he also saw the apparition in the wings wearing a beige coat and twill trousers.

The episode was related in the documentary produced by the television channel, though cameramen failed to capture images of the ghost itself.

Nigel Everett, a director of the theatre, said, 'Patrick told us all about it. He was stunned. I would not say frightened, but I would say impressed.' Appearances of Buckstone were not that frequent, Mr Everett said, with the last being by a stage hand about three or four years previous. He added, 'The last time an actor saw him would have been I think Fiona Fullerton, playing in an Oscar Wilde, ten or twelve years ago.' The ghost tends to appear when a comedy is playing.

While he said he did not consider *Waiting for Godot* to be a comedy, he thought their production did have comic aspects. 'I think Buckstone appears when he appreciates things,' he added. 'We view it as a positive thing.'

Others who have sighted the phantom include Dame Judi Dench and Sir Donald Sinden. The latter saw him when he was playing in *The Heiress* with Ralph Richardson in 1949.

However, like the other Theatre Royal's famous phantom, the 'Man in Grey', Buckstone is considered a good omen. The productions he visits are blessed with luck and a long run. But no need to worry; if you are not keen on spirits appearing while you're watching a show, he prefers to materialise in the dressing rooms and doesn't appear to the audience.

And so, our foray into London's haunted theatres in this book is over. According to superstition, a resident theatre ghost is a sign of good fortune – if this is true, there must be many auspicious theatres in London's West End. But it is as well to remember that when you next visit a West End theatre and sense a sudden cold breath of air, or imagine you feel an icy touch from a spidery hand, it probably isn't due to a breeze coming from an open exit door; it just might be the resident ghost.

BIBLIOGRAPHY AND SOURCES

Books

Ackroyd, P., *The English Ghost: Spectres Through Time* (London: Chatto & Windus, 2010)

Boswell, J. (ed. L.F. Powell), *Life of Johnson* (Oxford: Clarendon Press, 1934)

———, *A Sentimental Murder: Love and Madness in the Eighteenth Century* (New York: Farrar, Straus and Giroux, 2005)

Earl, J. and M. Sell, *Guide to British Theatres 1750–1950* (London: The Theatres Trust, 2000)

Frommer's 24 Great Walks in London (Barnes & Noble, 2011)

Hadley, P., *From Stage to Platform: The Metamorphosis of the Strand Theatre 1830–1905*, (London Passenger Transport 1984 No. 12, April)

Johnson, S., *The Ghost Map: A Street, an Epidemic and the Hidden Power of Urban Networks* (London: Penguin, 2008)

Lounsbury, W.C. and N. Boulanger, *Theatre Backstage from A to Z*, 3rd edition (Washington: University of Washington Press, 1989)

McKenzie, R., *They Still Serve: A Complete Guide to the Military Ghosts of Britain* (lulu.com, 2008)

Ogden, T., *Haunted Theatres: Playhouse Phantoms, Opera House Horrors and Backstage Banshees* (Guildford: Globe Pequot Press, 2009)

Olson, D., *London For Dummies* (USA: Wiley Publishing Inc., 2010)

Simpson, S., and J. Westwood, *The Penguin Book of Ghosts: Haunted England* (London: Penguin, 2005)

Pencer, J. and A., *The Encyclopedia of Ghosts and Spirits* (London: Headline, 1992)

Walford, E., *Old London: Strand to Soho* (London: The Alderman Press, 1987)

Willey, Russ, *Brewer's Dictionary of London Phrase and Fable* (Edinburgh: Chambers Harrap, 2012)

Newspapers and Periodicals:

Catholic Herald
Daily Mail
Daily Telegraph
Metro
The Guardian
The Independent
The Stage
Time Out

Websites:

www.arthurlloyd.co.uk
www.bl.uk
www.coventgarden.uk.com
www.haunted-london.com
www.information-britain.co.uk
www.london-ghost-tour.com
www.met.police.uk
www.mysteriousbritain.co.uk
www.onegoldensquare.com
www.paranormal-insight.ipbhost.com
www.russellgrant.com
www.slemen.com www.stage.co.uk
www.spookyisles.com
www.theshiptavern.co.uk
www.TheTravelMagazine.co.uk
www.ucl.ac.uk
www.ufofreeparanormal.com
www.uncannyuk.com
www.vam.ac.uk
www.walksoflondon.co.uk

Articles

'Apsley House and Park Lane' in *Old and New London: Volume 4* (1878) www.british-history.ac.uk

'Berkeley Square, North Side' in *Survey of London: Volume 40: The Grosvenor Estate in Mayfair, Part 2 (The Buildings)* (1980) www.british-history.ac.uk

'Berkeley Square and its Neighbourhood' in *Old and New London: Volume 4* (1878) at British History Online

'Montpelier Square Area: Montpelier Square' in *Survey of London: Volume 45: Knightsbridge* (2000) www.british-history.ac.uk

'Industries: Brewing' in *A History of the County of Middlesex: Volume 2* (1911) www.british-history.ac.uk

'The Pub With No Street Entrance' in *London Loop: 10* (2008)

'The Strand: Introduction' in *Old and New London: Volume 3* (1878) www.british-history.ac.uk

'Central Activities Zone' in *The London Plan: A Simple Plan*

'The Piazza: Nos. 1–4 (consec.) Little Piazza with 11 Russell Street' in *Survey of London: Volume 36: Covent Garden* (1970) www.british-history.ac.uk

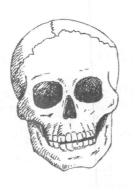

If you enjoyed this book, you may also be interested in …

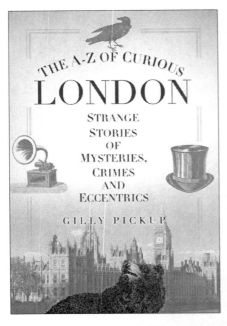

The A-Z of Curious London
GILLY PICKUP

Spooky, gruesome, weird but true things about one of the world's greatest cities come alive in *The A-Z of Curious London*. Discover London's tiniest house, a 4,000-year-old mouse made from Nile clay, and have a giggle at things people leave on London's transport (including false teeth, a human skull and a park bench – yes, really.) To sum up, eccentrics, legends, folklore, murders, scandals, ghosts, incredible characters and oodles of wow factor, it's all here.

978 0 7524 8968 1

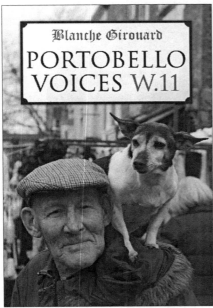

Portobello Voices
BLANCHE GIROUARD

Portobello Market has been going since 1860. It boasts the largest antiques street market in the world, is a source of inspiration for fashion designers, song writers and film directors, receives over a million visitors a year … and is at risk. In *Portobello Voices*, Blanche Girouard introduces us to the intoxicating mix of characters that make the market buzz – from the antique dealer to rubbish collector, sausage seller to fur coat vendor, Afghan battery seller to public school entrepreneur. Listening to their stories, learn how to spot a fake, store a fur and make a tin pan; find out what lies behind an obsession with collecting, a passion for buttons and the gusset in boxer shorts and hear how experiences of loss, abandonment and estrangement lead to a life as a market trader.

978 0 7524 9936 9

Visit our website and discover thousands of other History Press books.
www.thehistorypress.co.uk

The History Press

Lightning Source UK Ltd.
Milton Keynes UK
UKOW04f0730151013

219053UK00001B/24/P